What's In A Name?

For your namesake, don't guess! The name you choose for your baby will be a part of his or her identity for life. And whether you know it or not, it can affect his personality, popularity or even future business and professional success.

This book is specifically designed to assist you in making your greatest parental decision. Listed here are thousands of boys' and girls' names from which to choose—all alphabetized, all clearly defined. Only you will know the right name for your baby—and somewhere in this book you'll find it.

6000

NAMES

FOR

YOUR BABY

A DELL BOOK

Published by
Dell Publishing
a division of
Bantam Doubleday Dell Publishing Group, Inc.
666 Fifth Avenue
New York, New York 10103

This work is a new, expanded edition of
4000 Names for your Baby.

ISBN 0-440-17956-4

Printed in the United States of America

November 1983

20

RAD

CONTENTS

INTRODUCTION

A Rose by
Any Other Name . . .

is still a Rose, but if, by chance, Rose's last name were
Budd, Bush or Redd, she would probably daydream of
marriage even more fervently than most other young girls.
Why? Because Rose's parents would have left their daughter open to years of ridicule and teasing by ignoring a
cardinal rule of naming *any* baby:

*Resist the temptation to be humorous or cute when
matching a baby's given name to his or her surname.*

Fortunately, not many parents surrender to that temptation (though there *are* birth certificates that read "Ima
Stone" and "Forrest Green"), but, unfortunately, picking a
suitable name for baby isn't simply a matter of resisting the
impulse to be clever. Remember, the name you choose for
your baby will be a part of his or her identity for life; the
name you select can affect your baby's personality and
popularity (especially when he begins school), can color his
feelings toward himself, can even affect the degree of his
success in business or professional life. For example, the
name Robin (or worse, its diminutive form, Rob) Banks

would hardly be an asset to a young man aspiring to a career in finance or the law.

Be wary of names that are ultra-unique (you and/or baby may tire quickly of such a name) and, especially if baby is a boy, be certain to pick a name that leaves no doubt as to his sex—Jean and Joyce are popular, acceptable names for many European boys, but heaven help any American boy bearing either name!

Listen carefully to the sound and rhythm of the names you're considering for baby. Say the *full* name aloud, letting your ears, good judgment, and good taste guide you. Most people find that a surname of just one syllable—Jones, Smith, White, etc.—usually combines best with a given name of two or more syllables. For example, doesn't "Bethany Kent" have a softer, more lyrical sound than "Beth" or "Bess Kent"?

With surnames of two syllables—Carter, Hudson, Turner, etc.—try given names of three syllables, i.e., "Belinda Pauling," "Patricia Meaker." And with surnames of three syllables, experiment with given names of one or two syllables, i.e., "Ann Luellen," "Sally Cameron." As you try various names for baby, remember this general rule of rhythm and sound: a full name usually sounds most pleasant when the syllables of the given and surname are *un*equal in number.

Avoid unusual spellings of a name if it makes the name difficult to pronounce. No one wants to go through life hearing his name mispronounced and, perhaps worse, no one wants a name that new acquaintances are hesitant or embarrassed to say aloud. "Jon" is an easy way to vary the spelling of "John" (without changing the name's pronunciation), but you'd be wise not to vary "Alice" by spelling it "Alys"—unless you're unperturbed at the thought of your daughter often being called "Als" or "Alleys."

If your surname is simple, it's usually wise to keep baby's given name simple. You may be drawn to sophisticated names such as Jocelyn or Stephanie, but if your last name is Tead or Stubbs, the combination may sound humorous. In addition, keep in mind the national origin of your surname and of the given names you consider. For example, "Yvonne" and "Jacques" sound fine when combined with a surname such as "DuBrow," but awkward when matched with names such as "Kelly," "Cohen," or "Cappola."

Your religion may affect your choice of baby's name so— *before* you reach a decision—find out if your faith has any specific requirements or traditions regarding the naming of its children. For example, it's traditional that Jewish children are named for a beloved member of the family who is no longer alive, and it's required that Catholic children be given the name of a saint, either as a first or as a middle name. If you have any doubts about the customs or requirements of your faith, talk to your religious leader— *now.*

In this book are more than 5,500 names, plus their origins and their meanings. In order to be able to include as many names as possible, the following form has been used:

CAROLINE: (Teutonic) "one who is strong." Another feminine form of Charles. Var. and dim., Carola, Carolina, Carolyn, Karolima, Karoline, Karolyn; Carrie, Lina.

Translated, this means that the name "Caroline" is Teutonic in origin, that it means "one who is strong," and that it is one of the many feminine forms of the male name "Charles." "Carola," "Carolina," "Carolyn," "Karolima," "Karoline," and "Karolyn" are spelling *variants* (abbreviated "var.") of the name "Caroline." Its *diminutives,* which are derivative forms affectionately denoting something small or young (abbreviated "dim.") are "Carrie" and "Lina." Generally, variants are listed alphabetically immediately following the name, and a new alphabetical listing is begun for diminutives.

9

You will note that many common names are variants or diminutives of another name. "Eleanor" and "Nora," for example, are commonly accepted as names unto themselves. Technically, however, they are both derived from "Helen," since "Eleanor" is a variant of "Helen," and "Nora" is a diminutive of Eleanor.

Many of the names listed in this book are now antiquated; however, their variants and diminutives are often still popular. For example, you aren't likely to name your daughter "Tabitha" or "Tamara," but the diminutive of these names—"Tabbie" and "Tammy"—are names you may want to consider. So, don't skip over any of the names listed, and be sure to check all of the variants and diminutives. Somewhere in the pages of this book is the name that will best suit your precious new baby.

NAMES FOR

Girls

A

ABBEY, ABBIE, ABBY: *see* Abigail.

ABIGAIL: (Hebrew) "a source of joy." Var. and dim., Abbey, Abbie, Abby, Gael, Gail, Gale, Gayl.

ARBA: (Hebrew) a woman who represents the eternal mother of the world.

ACACIA: (Greek) "thorny."

ACANTHA: (Greek) "sharp-pointed."

ADA: (Teutonic) "joyous" or "prosperous." Var. and dim., Aida, Edna; Addie, Addy.

ADABELLE: Ada and Belle combined; thus, "joyous and fair." Var., Adabel.

ADAH: (Hebrew) "ornament."

ADALIA: (Old German) "noble one."

ADAMINA: (Latin) a feminine of Adam.

ADAR: (Hebrew) "fire."

ADELA, ADELE: *see* Adelaide.

ADELAIDE: (Teutonic) "noble and of kind spirit." Var. and dim., Adalia, Adaline, Adela, Adele, Adelia, Adelina, Adelind, Adeline, Adella, Adila, Dela, Della; plus all var. and dim. of Ada.

ADELINE: *see* Adelaide.

ADELPHA: (Greek) "sisterly."

ADIEL: (Hebrew) "ornament of the Lord." Var. and dim., Adiell; Addie, Addy.

ADINE: (Hebrew) "delicate." Feminine of Adin. Var., Adena, Adina.

ADNA: (Hebrew) "pleasure." Var., Adnah.

ADOLPHA: (Old German) feminine of Adolf.

ADONIA: (Greek) "godlike."

ADORA: (Teutonic) "the beloved; the adored."

ADORABELLE: (Latin-French) "beautiful gift."

ADRIA: (Latin) "dark one." *See also* Adrienne.

ADRIENNE: (Latin) "woman of the sea." Feminine of Adrian. Var., Adria, Adriana, Adriane, Adrianna, Adrianne.

AGATHA: (Greek) "good." Var. and dim., Agathe, Agathy, Ag, Aggie, Aggy.

AGAVE: (Greek) "noble."

AGNES: (Greek) "pure, chaste; gentle." Var. and dim., Agna, Agnella, Agneta, Nessa, Nessie, Neysa.

AIDA: *see* Ada.

AIDAN: (Irish Gaelic) "little fire."

AILEEN: (Greek) "light." Var., Aléne, Aline, Eileen, Ilene, Iline, Illene, Illona.

AILSA: (Teutonic) "girl of cheer."

AIMEE: (French) "beloved."

AIRLIA: (Greek) "of the air; ethereal."

AISLINN: (Irish Gaelic) "dream."

ALANA: (Celtic) "handsome" or "fair." Feminine of Alan. Var. and dim., Alina, Allana, Lana, Lane.

ALARICE: (Teutonic) "ruler of all." Feminine of Alaric. Var., Alarise.

ALBERTA: (Teutonic) "noble and brilliant." Feminine of Albert. Var and dim., Albertina, Albertine, Elberta; Bert, Berta, Bertie.

ALBINIA: (Latin) "white."

ALCINA: (Greek) "strong-minded."

ALDA: (Teutonic) "rich." *See also* Aldis.

ALDIS: (Old English) "from the oldest house." Var. and dim., Aldas, Aldya; Alda.

ALDORA: (Greek) "winged gift."

ALENE: *see* Aileen.

ALERIA: (Latin) "eaglelike."

ALETHEA: (Greek) "truth." Var. and dim., Aleta, Alitta, Letta, Thea.

ALEXANDRA: (Greek) "helper of mankind." Feminine of Alexander. Var. and dim., Alexa, Alexis, Alix, Alla, Elexa, Sandi, Sandra, Sondra.

ALEXIS: *see* Alexandra.

ALFONSINE: (Old German) Feminine of Alfonso.

ALFREDA: (Teutonic) "supernaturally wise." Feminine of Alfred. Dim., Ally.

ALICE: (Greek) "truth." Var. and dim., Aleece, Alicia, Alis, Alisa, Alison, Alissa, Allis, Alyce, Alys, Alysia, Alyssa, Elissa; Alla, Allie, Ally.

ALICIA, ALISSA: *see* Alice.

ALIDA: (Greek) "from the city of fine vestments." Var. and dim., Aleda, Alyda, Leda, Lida.

ALIMA: (Arabic) "learned in dancing and music."

ALISON: *see* Alice.

ALLEGRA: (Latin) "cheerful."

ALMA: (Latin) "cherishing."

ALMIRA: (Arabic) "princess; the exalted." Feminine of Elmer. Var. and dim., Elmira, Mira.

ALOHA: (Hawaiian) "welcome" or "farewell."

ALOYSE: *see* Aloysia.

ALOYSIA: (Teutonic) "famed battler." Feminine of Aloysius. Var. and dim., Aloisia, Aloyse, Lois.

ALPHA: (Greek) "first one."

ALTA: (Latin) "tall in spirit."

ALTHEA: (Greek) "wholesome; healing." Var. and dim., Althee, Altheta, Thea.

ALULA: (Latin) "winged one."

ALURA: (Old English) "divine counselor."

ALVA: (Latin) "white, fair."

ALVINA: (Teutonic) "beloved; friend of all." Feminine of Alvin. Dim., Vina.

ALZENA: (Arabic-Persian) "the woman."

AMABEL: (Latin) "lovable one."

AMANDA: (Latin) "lovable." Dim., Manda, Mandie, Mandy.

AMARIS: (Hebrew) "God has promised."

AMARYLLIS: (Latin) "the amaryllis lily."

AMBER: (Arabic) "jewel."

AMBROSINE: (Greek) feminine of Ambrose.

AMELIA: (Teutonic) "industrious, striving." A feminine form of Emil. Var. and dim., Amalia, Amelie, Melie, Mell, Mill, Millie. *See also* Emily.

AMELINDA: (Latin-Spanish) "beloved and pretty."

AMENA: (Celtic) "honest."

AMETHYST: (Greek) "wine-color."

AMITY: (Old French) "friendship."

AMY: (Latin) "beloved." Var., Aimee, Ami, Amie.

ANABEL, ANABELLA, ANABELLE: *see* Ann.

ANASTASIA: (Greek) "one who will rise again." Var. and dim., Ana, Stacey, Stacy.

ANATOLA: (Greek) "of the east." Feminine of Anatole.

ANDREA: (Italian) "womanly." Feminine of Andrew. Var. and dim., Andre, Andreana; Andee, Andi, Andy.

ANEMONE: (Greek) "wind flower."

ANGELA: (Greek) "heavenly messenger" or "angelic." Var. and dim., Angelica, Angelina, Angeline, Angelita; Angel, Angie, Angy.

ANGIE: *see* Angela.

ANITA: (Hebrew) "grace." A form (originally Spanish) of Ann.

ANN: (Hebrew) "full of grace, mercy, and prayer." Originally from the name Hannah. Var. and dim., Anabel, Anabella, Anabelle, Anna, Anne, Annetta, Annette, Annie, Annora, Anya, Nan, Nana, Nancy, Nanete, Nanette, Nanine, Nanon, Nina, Ninette, Ninon.

ANNETTE: *see* Ann.

ANNUNCIATA: (Latin) "bearer of news."

ANONA: (Latin) "yearly crops."

ANSELMA: (Teutonic) "the protectress." Dim., Selma.

ANTHEA: (Greek) "like a flower." Var. and dim., Anthia; Bluma, Thea, Thia.

16

ANTOINETTE: *see* Antonia.

ANTONIA: (Latin) "super-excellent." Feminine of Anthony. Var. and dim., Antoinetta, Antoinette, Antoni, Antonina, Netta, Nettie, Netty, Toinette, Toni.

ANYA: *see* Ann.

APHRODITE: (Greek) "goddess of love."

APOLLINE: (Greek) "sun or sunlight."

APRIL: (Latin) "to open" (as the earth opens in spring).

ARABELLA: (Latin) "fair and beautiful altar." Var. and dim., Arabelle; Ara, Bel, Bell, Bella, Belle.

ARDIS: (Latin) "fervent" or "zealous." Var., Ardelia, Ardelis, Ardella, Ardelle, Ardene, Ardine, Ardra.

ARDRA: *see* Ardis.

ARGENTA: (Latin) "silvery one."

ARIADNE: (Greek) "holy one." Var., Ariana, Ariane.

ARLENE: (Celtic) "a pledge." Var., Arlana, Arleen, Arlena, Arlette, Arlina, Arline.

ARMIDA: (Latin) "little armed one."

ARMILLA: (Latin) "bracelet."

ARMINA: (Old German) "warrior maid." Var., Armine, Erminie.

ARNALDA: (Old German) Feminine of Arnold.

ASELMA: (Old Norse) "protection."

ASTRA: (Greek) "like a star." Var., Astrea, Astred, Astrid.

ATALANTA: (Greek) "mighty bearer."

ATALAYA: (Spanish) "guardian."

ATHENA: (Greek) "wise; wisdom." Var., Athene.

AUDREY: (English) "strong, noble." Var. and dim., Audrie, Audry; Audie, Dee.

AUGUSTA: (Latin) "majestic, sacred." Feminine of August. Var. and dim., Augustina, Augustine; Austina, Austine, Gussie, Gusta, Tina.

AURELIA: (Latin) "golden." Var., Aura, Aurea, Aurelie, Aurora; Aurel, Aurie, Ora, Oralia, Oralie, Orel.

AURORA: *see* Aurelia.

AVA: *see* Avis.

AVIS: (Latin) "a bird." Var. and dim., Ava, Avi.

AZALIA: (Hebrew) "whom the Lord reserved." Var., Azalea, Azelia.

AZURA: (Old French) "blue sky."

B

BABETTE: *see* Barbara.

BALBINA: (Latin-Italian) "little stammerer."

BARBARA: (Greek) "mysterious stranger." Var. and dim., Babette, Barbette; Babby, Babs, Barby, Bobbi, Bobbie.

BASILIA: (Greek) "regal."

BATHILDA: (Old German) a girl who fought for honor and truth.

BATHSHEBA: (Hebrew) "the daughter of our oath." Dim., Sheba.

BEATA: (Latin) "blessed; divine." Dim., Bea.

BEATRICE: (Latin) "she brings joy." Var. and dim., Beautrix; Bea, Bee, Trix, Trixie.

BECKY: *see* Rebecca.

BEDA: (Old English) "warrior maiden."

BELINDA: (Italian) "wise and immortal." Dim., Bel, Linda, Lindie, Lindy.

BELLA, BELLE: *see* Arabella, Isabel, Mabel, etc.

BELLANCA: (Italian) "blond one."

BENA: (Hebrew) "wise." Var., Benay.

BENEDICTA: (Latin) "one who is blessed." Feminine of Benedict. Var., Benedetta, Benetta, Benita.

BENIGNA: (Latin) "kind, gracious, gentle."

BENITA: *see* Benedicta.

BERENGARIA: (Old English) "bear–spear maid."

BERNADETTE: *see* Bernadine.

18

BERNADINE: (Teutonic) "brave; strong." Feminine of Bernard. Var. and dim., Bernadette, Bernadina; Berneta, Bernetta, Bernette, Berni, Bernie.

BERNIA: (Old Anglo-Latin) "battle maid."

BERNICE: (Greek) "she brings victory." Var. and dim., Berenice; Berni, Berny.

BERTHA: (Teutonic) "shining, bright." Var. and dim., Berta, Bertina; Berti, Bertie.

BERTILDE: (Old English) "shining battle maid."

BERTRADE: (Old English) "shining counselor."

BERYL: (Hebrew) "jewel; precious." Var. and dim., Beryle; Berri, Berrie, Berry.

BESS, BESSE, BESSIE: *see* Elizabeth.

BETH: (Hebrew) "place" or "house of God." *See also* Elizabeth.

BETHSEDA: (Hebrew) "house of mercy."

BETSY, BETTE, BETTINA, BETTY: *see* Elizabeth.

BEULAH: (Hebrew) "she who will be married."

BEVERLY: (Anglo-Saxon) "beaver-meadow." Var. and dim., Beverley, Beverlie; Bev, Bevvy.

BEVIN: (Irish Gaelic) "melodious lady."

BIANCA, BLANCA: *see* Blanche.

BILLIE: (Teutonic) "wise protector." A feminine diminutive of William. Var., Bille.

BINA: *see* Sabina.

BINGA: (Old German) "from the kettle-shaped hollow."

BIRDIE: a modern name; "sweet little bird."

BLANCHE: (French) "fair; white." Var., Bianca, Blanca, Blanch, Branca.

BLASIA: (Latin) "stammerer."

BLESSING: (Old English) "consecrated one."

BLISS: (Old English) "gladness, joy." *See also* Blythe.

BLOSSOM: (Old English) "fresh, lovely."

BLUMA: *see* Anthea.

BLYTHE: (Anglo-Saxon) "blithe; happy." Var., Bliss, Blisse.

BOBBI, BOBBIE: *see* Barbara, Roberta.

BONITA: (Spanish) "pretty."

BONNIE: (Latin) "sweet and good." Var., Boni, Bonne, Bonni, Bonny.

BRENDA: (Teutonic) "fiery." Dim., Bren.

BRENNA: (Celtic) "maiden with black or raven hair."

BRIDGET: (Celtic) "mighty; strong." Var. and dim., Bridgid, Brigette, Brigida, Brigitte; Brieta, Brietta, Brita, Brie.

BRIGETTE, BRIGITTE: *see* Bridget.

BRINA: *see* Sabrina, Zabrina.

BRONWEN: (Old Welsh) "white-bossomed."

BRUCIE: (Old French) "from the thicket."

BRUNHILDE: (Teutonic) "heroine on the battlefield." Var., Brunhild, Brunhilda.

BRYNA: (Irish Gaelic) "strength, virtue, honor."

C

CADENCE: (Latin) "rhythmic."

CALANDRA: (Greek) "lark."

CALANTHA: (Greek) "beautiful blossom."

CALENDONIA: (Latin) "from Scotland."

CALIDA: (Spanish) "warm, ardent."

CALISTA: (Greek) "most beautiful one."

CALLA: (Greek) "beautiful."

CALLULA: (Latin) "little beautiful one."

CALTHA: (Latin) "yellow flower."

CALVINA: (Latin) "bald." Feminine of Calvin.

CALYPSO: (Greek) "concealer."

CAMEO: (Italian) "a sculptured jewel."

CAMILLA: (Latin) "noble; righteous." Var. and dim., Camella, Camellia, Camille; Cam, Milly.

CAMILLE: *see* Camilla.

CANACE: (Greek) "daughter of the wind."

CANDACE: (Latin) "pure; glowing fire-white." Var. and dim., Candice; Candida; Candie, Candy.

CAPRICE: (Italian) "fanciful."

CARA: (Celtic) "friend."

CARESSE: (French) "endearing one."

CARISSA: *see* Charissa.

CARITA: (Latin) "beloved, dear one."

CARLA: (Teutonic) "one who is strong." A feminine form of Charles. Var. and dim., Karla; Carly, Karly.

CARLOTTA: (Italian) "one who is strong." Another feminine form of Charles. *See also* Charlotte.

CARMA: (Sanskrit) "fate or destiny."

CARMEL: (Hebrew) "God's fruitful field." Var., Carmela, Carmelita.

CARMEN: (Latin) "a song." Var. and dim., Carmena, Carmina, Carmine, Carmita.

CARNATION: (French) "flesh color."

CAROL: (French) "joyous song." Var. and dim., Carole, Carolle, Caryl, Karol, Karole; Carey, Carrie, Cary.

CAROLINE: (Teutonic) "one who is strong." Another feminine form of Charles. Var. and dim., Carola, Carolina, Carolyn, Karolina, Karoline, Karolyn; Carrie, Lina.

CARRIE: *see* Carol, Caroline, Charlotte.

CASSANDRA: (Greek) "the prophetess." Var. and dim., Cassandre; Cass, Cassie.

CASTA: (Latin) "pure, pious, modest one."

CATHARINE, CATHERINA, CATHERINE, CATHLEEN: *see* Katherine.

CECILIA: (Latin) "musical." Feminine of Cecil. Var. and dim., Cecile, Cecily, Celia, Cicily, Cis, Cissy.

CELANDINE: (Greek) "the swallow."

CELESTE: (Latin) "heavenly." Var., Celesta, Celestine.

CELIA: *see* Cecilia.

CELOSIA: (Greek) "flaming, burning."

CEPORAH: *see* Zipporah.

CERELIA: (Latin) "of the spring."

CHANDRA: (Sanskrit) "she outshines the stars."

CHARISSA: (Greek) "graceful." Var., Carissa.

CHARITY: (Latin) "charitable; loving." Var. and dim., Charita; Charry, Cherry.

CHARLENE, CHARLINE: *see* Charlotte.

CHARLOTTE: (Teutonic) "strong; womanly." Another feminine form of Charles. Var. and dim., Carlotta, Charlene, Charline; Carry, Carrie, Letty, Lotta, Lotte, Lottie, Lotty.

CHARMAINE: (Latin) "little song." Var., Charmain.

CHERIE: (French) "dear one." Var., Cheryl, Sheryl, Sherry.

CHERRY: (Old North French) "cherrylike." *See also* Charity.

CHERYL: *see* Cherie.

CHIQUITA: (Spanish) "little one."

CHLOE: (Greek) "fresh blooming." Var., Cloe.

CHRISTABEL, CHRISTABELLE: *see* Christine.

CHRISTINE: (Greek) "fair Christian." Feminine of Christian. Var. and dim., Christa, Christabel, Christabelle, Christal, Christiana, Christina, Chrystal, Crystal, Kristiana, Kristina, Kristine; Chris, Chrissie, Chrissy, Teena, Tina, Xina.

CICILY, CIS, CISSY: *see* Cecilia.

CINDY: *see* Cynthia.

CLAIRE, CLARE: *see* Clara.

CLARA: (Latin) "bright; shining." Var., Claire, Clare, Clareta, Clarette, Clarine.

CLARABELLE: (Latin-French) "bright, shining; beautiful." Var., Claribel.

CLARISSA: (Latin) "one who will be famous." Var., Clarice, Clarisa, Clarise.

CLAUDETTE: *see* Claudia.

CLAUDIA: (Latin) "the lame" (this meaning has been obscured by time and usage). Feminine of Claud. Var. and dim., Claude, Claudette, Claudina, Claudine, Claudie.

CLEMATIS: (Greek) "vine or brushwood."

CLEMENTIA: (Latin) "mild, calm, merciful."

CLEMENTINE: (Latin) "mild; kind; merciful." Feminine of Clement.

CLEO: *see* Cleopatra.

CLEOPATRA: (Greek) "of a famous father." Dim., Cleo.

CLEVA: (Middle English) "dweller at the cliff."

CLIANTHA: (Greek) "glory-flower."

CLIO: (Greek) "the proclaimer."

CLOE: *see* Chloe.

CLOTILDE: (Teutonic) "famous battle maiden." Var., Clothilde, Clotilda.

CLOVER: (Old English) "clover blossom."

CLYMENE: (Greek) "renowned, famed one."

CLYTIE: (Greek) "splendid or beautiful one."

COLETTE: (Latin) "victorious." Var., Collette.

COLLEEN: (Irish) "girl." Var., Coleen, Colene.

COLUMBIA: (Latin) "the dove."

COMFORT: (French) "strengthening aid and comfort."

CONCEPTION: (Latin) "beginning."

CONCORDIA: (Latin) "harmony."

CONRADINE: (Old German) "bold, wise counselor."

CONSTANCE: (Latin) "unchanging; constant." Var. and dim., Constantia, Constantina, Constantine; Con, Conni, Connie.

CONSUELA: (Latin) "consolation." Var. and dim., Consuelo; Connie.

CORA: (Greek) "maiden." Var. and dim., Corene, Coretta, Corette, Corinna, Corinne, Correna, Corrie, Corry.

CORAL: (Greek) "from the sea coral." Var. and dim., Koral; Coralie.

23

CORDELIA: (Celtic) "the sea's jewel." Var. and dim., Cordellia; Delia, Della.

CORINNA, CORINNE: *see* Cora.

CORNELIA: (Latin) "womanly virtue." Feminine of Cornelius. Var. and dim., Cornela, Nelia, Nell, Nellie.

COSIMA: (Greek) "Order, harmony; the world."

CRESCENT: (Old French) "to increase or create."

CRISPINA: (Latin) "curly-haired."

CRYSTAL: *see* Christine.

CYNARA: (Greek) "thistle or artichoke."

CYNTHIA: (Greek) "moon goddess." Dim., Cindy, Cyn, Cynth, Cynthie.

CYPRIS: (Greek) "from the island of Cyprus."

CYRENA: (Greek) "from Cyrene."

CYRILLA: (Latin) "lordly one."

CYTHEREA: (Greek) "from the island of Cythera."

D

DACIA: (Greek) "from Dacia."

DAFFODIL: (Old French) "the daffodil flower."

DAGMAR: (Danish) "joy of the land." Dim,. Dag.

DAHLIA: (Old Norse) "from the valley."

DAISY: (Anglo-Saxon) "the day's eye." Var., Daisie.

DALE: (Teutonic) "dweller in the valley." Var., Dail, Daile.

DAMARA: (Greek) "gentle girl." Var. and dim., Damaris; Mara.

DAMITA: (Spanish) "little noble lady."

DANICA: (Old Slavic) "star; morning star."

DANIELA: (Hebrew) feminine of Daniel.

DAPHNE: (Greek) "laurel tree." Dim., Daph, Daphie.

DARCIE: (French-Celtic) "from the stronghold; dark one." Var., Dara.

DARDA: (Hebrew) "pearl of wisdom." Var., Dara.

DARICE: (Persian) "queenlike." Var. and dim., Dareece, Darees; Dari.

DARLENE: (Anglo-Saxon) "dearly beloved." Var. and dim., Darleen, Darline, Daryl.

DAVINA: (Hebrew) "the loved." Feminine of David. Var., Daveta, Davida, Davita.

DAWN: (Anglo-Saxon) "the break of day."

DEANNA: *see* Diana.

DEBORAH: (Hebrew) "the bee." Var. and dim., Debora, Debra; Deb, Debbie, Debby.

DEBRA: *see* Deborah.

DECIMA: (Latin) "the tenth daughter."

DEE: *see* Audrey, Deidre, Dorothy.

DEIDRE: (Gaelic) "sorrow." Var. and dim., Dierdre; Dee, Deedee.

DELIA: (Greek) "from the isle of Delos." *See also* Cordelia.

DELICIA: (Latin) "delightful one."

DELIGHT: (Old French) "delight of pleasure."

DELILAH: (Hebrew) "the temptress." Var. and dim., Dalila; Lila.

DELLA: (Teutonic) "of nobility." Dim., Del. *See also* Adelaide, Cordelia.

DELPHINE: (Greek) "calmness; serenity." Var., Delphinia.

DELTA: (Greek) fourth letter of the Greek alphabet.

DEMETRIA: (Greek) "from a fertile land." Var. and dim., Demitria, Dimitria; Demy.

DENA: (Old English) feminine of Dean.

DENISE: (Greek) "wine goddess." Feminine of Dennis. Var., Denice, Denys.

DESDEMONA: (Greek) "girl of sadness." Var. and dim., Desdamona; Demona, Mona.

DESIREE: (Latin-French) "so long hoped for."

DESMA: (Greek) "a bond or pledge."

DEVA: (Sanskrit) "divine."

DEVONA: (Old English) "from Devonshire."

DEXTRA: (Latin) "skillful, dexterous." Feminine of Dexter.

DIAMANTA: (French) "diamondlike."

DIANA: (Latin) "pure goddess of the moon." Var. and dim., Deanna, Diane, Dianna; Di.

DIANE: *see* Diana.

DIANTHA: (Greek) "flower of Zeus; divine flower."

DIDO: (Greek) "teacher."

DINAH: (Hebrew) "judged; exonerated." Var., Dina.

DIONE: (Greek) "the daughter of heaven and earth."

DISA: (Old Norse) "active sprite."

DIXIE: (American) "girl of the South." Dim., Dix.

DOANNA: American compound of Dorothy and Anna.

DOCILA: (Latin) "gentle, teachable."

DODI: *see* Doris.

DOLLEY, DOLLIE, DOLLY: *see* Dorothy.

DOLORES: (Latin) "our lady of sorrows." Var. and dim., Delores, Deloris, Dolora; Dori, Dorrie, Dorry.

DOMINA: (Latin) "lady."

DOMINICA: (Latin) "born on the Lord's day." Feminine of Dominic. Var., Dominique.

DOMINIQUE: *see* Dominica.

DONALDA: feminine of Donald.

DONATA: (Latin) "donation; gift."

DONNA: (Italian) "lady." Var., Dona.

DORA: (Greek) "a gift." *See also* Dorothy, Eudora, Isadora, etc.

DORCAS: (Greek) "a gazelle."

DORE: (French) "golden one."

DORENE: (French) "golden girl." Var. and dim., Doreen, Dorine; Dori, Dorie, Dorrie, Dorry.

DORI, DORIE, DORRIE, DORRY: *see* Dolores, Dorene, Dorinda, Isadora, Pandora, Theodora.

DORINDA: (Greek) "bountiful gift." Dim., Dori, Dorin.

DORIS: (Greek) "sea goddess." Dim., Dodi.

DOROTHY: (Greek) "God's gift." A feminine form of Theodore. Var. and dim., Dora, Doretta, Dorothea, Dorothi, Dorthea, Dorthy; Dee, Dolly, Dollie, Dolly, Dore, Dot, Dottie, Dotty.

DOTTIE, DOTTY: *see* Dorothy.

DRUELLA: (Old German) "elfin vision."

DRUSILLA: (Greek) "soft-eyed." Var. and dim., Drucilla; Dru, Drus, Drusie.

DUANA: (Irish Gaelic) "little dark one."

DUENA: (Spanish) "chaperon."

DULCIE: (Latin) "charming; sweet." Var., Dulci, Dulcine.

E

EARLENE: (Old English) feminine of Earl.

EARTHA: *see* Hertha.

EASTER: (Old English) "born at Easter time."

EBBA: (Old English) "flowing back of the tide."

ECHO: (Greek) "reflected sound."

EDA: (Old English) "prosperity, blessedness."

EDANA: (Irish Gaelic) "little fiery one."

EDE: (Greek) "generation."

EDEN: (Hebrew) "enchanting."

EDIE: *see* Edith.

EDINA: (Scotch) "from the city of Edinburgh."

EDITH: (Teutonic) "rich gift." Var. and dim., Eadith, Eda, Edythe; Eadie, Ede, Edie, Edina.

EDLYN: (Anglo-Saxon) "of nobil'ty." Dim., Lyn.

EDMONDA: (Old English) feminine of Edmund.

EDNA: (Hebrew) "rejuvenation." Dim., Edny. *See also* Ada.

EDREA: (Old English) "properous, powerful."

EDWINA: (Anglo-Saxon) "valued friend." A feminine form of Edwin. Var. and dim., Eadwina, Eadwine, Edwine; Win, Wina, Winnie, Winny.

EFFIE: (Greek) "fair and famed." Var., Effy. *See also* Euphemia.

EGLANTINE: (Old French) "sweetbrier rose; woodbine."

EILEEN: *see* Aileen.

EIR: (Old Norse) "peace, clemency."

ELAINE: (Greek) "light." Var. and dim., Alaine, Alayne, Elana, Elayne; Laine, Lani.

ELATA: (Latin) "lofty, elevated."

ELBERTA: *see* Alberta.

ELDORA: (Spanish) "gilded one."

ELDRIDA: (Old English) "old, wise counselor."

ELEANOR, ELEANORA, ELEANORE, ELENORE, ELINOR, ELINORE: *see* Helen.

ELECTRA: (Greek) "shining star." Dim., Lectra.

ELENA: *see* Helen.

ELEXA: *see* Alexandra.

ELFREDA: (Teutonic) "noble and wise." Feminine of Albert. Var., Elfrida.

ELGA: (Gothic) "holy, consecrated."

ELISE: *see* Elizabeth.

ELISSA: *see* Alice.

ELITA: (Latin) "select; a special person."

ELIZA: *see* Elizabeth.

ELIZABETH: (Hebrew) "consecrated to God." Var. and dim., Elisa, Elisabeth, Elisabetta, Elise, Eliza, Elsa, Elsbeth, Else, Elsie, Lisabet, Lisabeth, Lisbeth; Bess, Besse, Bessie, Beth, Betsy, Bette, Betti, Bettina, Betty, Libby, Lisa, Lise, Liz, Liza, Lizzie, Lizzy.

ELLA, ELLIE: *see* Helen.

ELLAMAY: compound of Ella and May.

ELLEN: *see* Helen.

ELLICE: (Greek) feminine of Elias.

ELMA: (Greek) "pleasant."

ELMIRA: *see* Almira.

ELOISE: *see* Louise.

ELSA, ELSIE: *see* Elizabeth.

ELVINA: (Old English) "elfin friend."

ELVIRA: (Spanish) "like an elf." Dim., Elva, Elvie.

ELYSIA: (Latin) "sweetly blissful."

EMERALD: (Old French) "the bright green emerald gem."

EMILIA: *see* Emily.

EMILY: (Teutonic) "industrious." A feminine form of Emil. Var. and dim., Emilia, Emilie, Em, Emmy, Millie. *See also* Amelia.

EMMA: (Teutonic) "one who heals." Dim., Em, Emie, Emmie, Emmy.

ENA: (Irish Gaelic) "little ardent or fiery one."

ENDORA: (Hebrew) "fountain."

ENGELBERTA: (Old German) "bright angel."

ENID: (Celtic) "purity of soul."

ENNEA: (Greek) "wine."

EOLANDE: *see* Yolande.

ERANTHE: (Greek) "spring flower."

ERDA: *see* Hertha.

ERICA: (Scandinavian) "of royalty." Feminine of Eric. Var. and dim., Erika; Rica, Ricky, Rika, Riki.

ERINA: (Celtic) "girl from Ireland." Var., Erin.

ERMA: *see* Irma.

ERNESTINE: (Teutonic) "earnest; purposeful." Feminine of Ernest. Var. and dim., Erna, Ernesta, Teena, Tina.

EDWINA: (Old English) A feminine form of Edwin.

ESMERALDA: (Greek) "emerald." Var. and dim., Ezmeralda; Esme.

ESTA: (Italian) "from the east." *See also* Vesta.

ESTELLE: (Latin) "a star." Var. and dim., Estella; Stella.

ESTHER: (Hebrew) "a star." Var. and dim., Esta, Ester; Essie, Essy.

ETHEL: (Teutonic) "noble." Var., Ethyl.

ETHELOEAN: modern compound of Ethel and Jean.

ETHELINDA: (Old German) "noble serpent."

29

ETTA: *see* Henrietta.

EUCLEA: (Greek) "glory."

EUDOCIA: (Greek) "of good repute."

EUDORA: (Greek) "wonderful gift." Dim., Dora.

EUGENIA: (Greek) "well born." Feminine of Eugene. Var. and dim., Eugenie; Gena, Gene, Genie, Gina.

EULALIA: (Greek) "fair speech; well-spoken one."

EUNICE: (Greek) "gloriously victorious."

EUPHEMIA: (Greek) "fair and famed." Var. and dim., Euphemie; Effie.

EURYDICE: (Greek) "broad separation."

EUSTACIA: (Latin) "stable, tranquil."

EVA: *see* Eve.

EVADNE: (Greek) "fortunate."

EVANGELINE: (Greek) "bearer of good news."

EVE: (Hebrew) "life" or "living." Var. and dim., Eva, Eveleen, Evelina, Eveline, Evelyn, Evita, Evonne; Evie.

EVELYN: *see* Eve.

EVONNE: *see* Eve.

F

FABIA: (Latin) feminine of Fabian.

FAITH: (Latin) "trusting; faithful." Var., Fae, Fay, Faye.

FANCHON: (French) "free."

FANNY: (Teutonic) "free." Var., Fan, Fannie.

FAUSTINA: (Latin) "very lucky." Var., Faustena, Faustine.

FAUSTINE: (Latin) "lucky, auspicious."

FAVOR: (Old French) "help, approval."

FAWN: (Old French) "young deer; reddish-brown colored."

FAY, FAYE: *see* Faith.

FAYANNE: compound of Fay and Anne.

FAYETTE: (Old French) "little fairy."

FAYME: (Old French) "lofty reputation."

FEALTY: (Old French) "fidelity, allegiance."

FELDA: (Old German) "from the field."

FELICIA: (Latin) "happy." Feminine of Felix. Var., Felice, Felise.

FENELLA: (Irish Gaelic) "white-shouldered one."

FERN: (Greek) "a feather."

FERNANDA: (Gothic) feminine of Ferdinand.

FIDELA: (Latin) "faithful woman." Var. and dim., Fidelia, Fidella; Fidelity.

FIFI: *see* Josephine.

FILMA: (Old English) "a veil or mist."

FIONA: (Irish Gaelic) "fair one."

FIONNA: (Celtic) "ivory-skinned." Var. and dim., Fiona, Phiona, Viona, Vionna; Fio.

FLANNA: (Irish Gaelic) "red-haired."

FLAVIA: (Latin) "yellow-haired; blond."

FLETA: (Old English) "swift, fleet one."

FLEUR, FLEURETTE, FLORA: *see* Florence.

FLORENCE: (Latin) "to flower and bloom." Var. and dim., Fleur, Fleurette, Flora, Florette, Floria, Floris, Flower; Flo, Flossie.

FLOWER: (Old French) "a blossom." *See also* Florence.

FONDA: (Middle English) "affectionate, tender."

FORTUNE: (Latin) "fate, destiny."

FRANCES: (Teutonic) "free." Feminine of Francis. Var. and dim., France, Francesca, Francine; Fran, Franny.

FREDA: (Teutonic) "peace." A feminine form of Frederick. Var. and dim., Freida, Frida, Frieda; Fredie. *See also* Wilfreda.

FREDERICA: (Teutonic) "peaceful." Another feminine form of Frederick. Var. and dim., Fredrica, Fredrika; Ricky.

31

FRITZIE: (Teutonic) "peaceful ruler." Feminine of Fritz. Var., Fritzi, Fritzy.

FRONDE: (Latin) "a leafy branch."

FULVIA: (Latin) "tawny or yellow-colored."

G

GABEY, GABIE: *see* Gabrielle.

GABRIELLE: (Hebrew) "woman of God." Feminine of Gabriel. Var. and dim., Gabriella; Gabey, Gabi, Gabie.

GAEA: (Greek) "the earth."

GAIL, GALE: *see* Abigail.

GALATEA: (Greek) "milky white."

GARDENIA: (Latin) "the fragrant white gardenia flower."

GARLAND: (Old French) "a wreath of flowers."

GARNET: (Teutonic) "radiant red jewel."

GAY: (origin uncertain) "merry." Var., Gae, Gaye.

GAZELLA: (Latin) "gazelle or antelope."

GELASIA: (Greek) "included to laughter."

GEMINI: (Greek) "twin." Var., Gemina.

GEMMA: (Italian) "a gem or precious stone."

GENA, GENE: *see* Eugenia.

GENEVIEVE: (Celtic) "white; pure." Var., Geneva.

GEORGETTE: *see* Georgiana.

GEORGIANA: (Greek) "earth-lover." Feminine of George. Var. and dim., Georgetta, Georgette, Georgia, Georgianna, Georgina, Georgine; Georgi, Georgie.

GERALDINE: (Teutonic) "ruler with a spear." Feminine of Gerald. Var. and dim., Geralda, Jeraldine; Geri, Gerri, Gerry, Jerri, Jerrie, Jerry.

GERANIUM: (Greek) "the geranium flower."

GERDA: (Teutonic) "the protected." Var. and dim., Garda, Gerdi.

GERMAIN: (French) "a German."

GERTRUDE: (Teutonic) "spear maiden." Dim., Gerta, Gerti, Gertie, Gerty, Trude, Trudy.

GILBERTA: (Teutonic) "the bright pledge." Feminine of Gilbert. Var. and dim., Gilberte, Gilbertine, Gilbertina.

GILDA: (Celtic) "God's servant." Dim., Gilli.

GILLIAN: (Latin) "youthful, downy-haired one."

GINA: *see* Eugenia, Regina.

GINGER, GINNY: *see* Virginia.

GISELLE: (Teutonic) "a promise." Var., Gisela, Gisele.

GITTEL: (Hebrew) "maiden of the winepress." Var., Gitel, Gitle, Gittle.

GLADYS: (Latin) "frail; delicate." Var. and dim., Gladine, Gladis; Glad, Gladdie.

GLENDA: *see* Glenna.

GLENNA: (origin uncertain) "from the valley." Feminine of Glenn. Var. and dim., Glenda, Glennis, Glynis; Glen, Glenn, Glennie.

GLORIA: (Latin) "the glorious." Dim., Glory.

GLORIANA: Gloria and Anna combined; thus, "glorious grace." Var., Glorianna.

GLYNIS: *see* Glenna.

GODIVA: (Old English) "gift of God."

GOLDIE: (Teutonic) "the golden-haired one." Var., Goldy.

GRACE: (Latin) "the graceful." Var. and dim., Gracia; Gracie, Gracye.

GREDEL, GRETA, GRETCHEN: *see* Margaret.

GREER: (Greek) "the watchwoman."

GREGORIA: (Latin) "watchful one."

GRISELDA: (Teutonic) "the heroine." Dim., Grissel, Selda, Zelda.

GUIDA: (Italian) "a guide."

GUINEVERE: (Celtic) "fair lady." Var. and dim., Guenevere, Jennifer; Gen, Genny, Jen, Jenni, Jennie, Jenny.

GUSTA: *see* Augusta.

GWENDOLEN: (Celtic) "white-browed." Var. and dim., Gwendolyn; Gwen, Gwenn, Gwyn, Gwyneth, Wendi, Wendy.

GYPSY: (of undetermined origin) "wanderer."

GYTHA: (Old English) "a gift."

H

HAGAR: (Hebrew) "one who flees." Var., Haggar.

HAIDEE: (Greek) "modest; honored."

HALCYONE: (Greek) "sea-conceived."

HALDANA: (Old Norse) "half Danish."

HALFRIDA: (Old German) "peaceful heroine."

HALIMEDA: (Greek) "thinking of the sea."

HANNAH: (Hebrew) "full of grace, mercy, and prayer." For Var. and dim., *see* Ann.

HAPPY: a modern name; "a happy child; joyful."

HARALDA: (Old Norse) "army ruler."

HARMONY: (Latin) "concord, harmony."

HARRIET: (Teutonic) "mistress of the home." A feminine form of Henry. Var. and dim., Harrietta, Harriette; Hatti, Hattie, Hatty.

HATTIE, HATTY: *see* Harriet.

HAZEL: (Anglo-Saxon) "authority or commander."

HEATHER: (Anglo-Saxon) "a flower." Dim., Heath.

HEBE: (Greek) "youth."

HEDDA: (Teutonic) "war." Var., Hedy, Heddy.

HEDWIG: (Teutonic) "storm; strife." Var. and dim., Hedvig, Edvig; Hedi.

HEIDI: *see* Hilda.

HELEN: (Greek) "light." Var. and dim., Helena, Helene, Hellene, Eleanor, Eleanora, Eleanore, Elena, Elene, Elenore, Elinor, Elinore, Ella, Ellen, Elnore, Lena,

Lenore, Leonora, Leonore, Leora, Lora, Lorine; Ellie, Lenni, Lennie, Nell, Nellie, Nelly, Nora.

HELGA: (Teutonic) "holy."

HELICE: (Greek) "special."

HELMA: (OLd German) "helmet or protection."

HELOISE: *see* Louise.

HELSA: (Hebrew) "given to God."

HENNI, HENNIE: *see* Henrietta.

HENRIETTA: (Teutonic) "mistress of the home." Another feminine form of Henry. Var. and dim., Henriette, Henrika; Etta, Etty, Henni, Hennie, Hetti, Hetty.

HEPHZIBAH: (Hebrew) "my joy is in her." Var. and dim., Hepsiba, Hepsibah; Hepsibetha.

HERA: (Greek) "queen of the gods."

HERMIONE: (Greek) "of the earth." Feminine of Herman.

HERMOSA: (Spanish) "beautiful."

HERTHA: (Teutonic) "earth mother." Var., Eartha, Erda, Herta.

HESPER: (Greek) "night star."

HESTER: (Persian) "a star." Dim., Hetti, Hettie, Hetty.

HETTI, HETTIE, HETTY: *see* Henrietta, Hester.

HIBERNIA: (Latin) "Ireland."

HIBISCUS: (Latin) "the marshmallow plant and flower."

HILARY: (Latin) "cheerful." Var., Hillarey, Hillary.

HILDA: (Teutonic) "battle maiden." Var. and dim., Heidi, Hilde; Hildie, Hildy.

HILDEGARD: (Teutonic) "battle maiden." Var. and dim., Hildagard, Hildagarde, Hilde; plus all dim. of Hilda.

HOLDA: (Old German) "concealed."

HOLLY: (Anglo-Saxon) "good luck." Var., Hollie.

HONEY: *see* Honora.

HONORA: (Latin) "honorable." Var. and dim., Honey, Honoria; Nora, Norah, Noreen, Norine, Norrie.

HOPE: (Anglo-Saxon) "optimistic and cheerful."

HORATIA: (Latin) "keeper of the hours."

HORTENSE: (Latin) "garden worker." Var., Hortensa.
HUBERTA: (Old German) Feminine of Hubert.
HUETTE: (Old English) Feminine of Hugh.
HULDA: (Old German) "gracious or beloved."
HYACINTH: (Greek) "hyacinth flower or purple hyacinth color."
HYPATIA: (Greek) "highest."

I

IANTHE: (Greek) "purple-colored flower." Dim., Ian.
IDA: (Teutonic) "happy." Var., Idalla, Idelle.
IDELIA: (Teutonic) "noble."
IDELLE: *see* Ida.
IDUNA: (Old Norse) "lover."
IGNACIA: (Latin) "ardent." Feminine of Ignatius. Var., Ignatia, Ignatzia.
IGNATIA: (Latin) "fiery, ardent one."
ILA: (Old French) "from the island."
ILENNA: (Greek) "from the city of Ilion or Troy."
ILENE, ILINE, ILLENE, ILLONA: *see* Aileen.
ILKA: (Celtic) "hard worker."
ILONA: (Hungarian) "beautiful one."
ILSA, ILSE: var. of Elsa; thus, *see* Elizabeth.
IMOGENE: (Latin) "an image." Var., Imogen.
IMPERIA: (Latin) "imperial one."
INA: *see* Katherine.
INEZ: (Greek) "chaste; pure; gentle." Var., Ines.
INGA: *see* Ingrid.
INGRID: (Swedish) "daughter." Var., Inga, Ingeborg.
INIGA: (Latin) "fiery, ardent one."
IOLA: (Greek) "dawn cloud; violet color."
IOLANTHE: (Greek) "violet flower."

IONA: (Greek) "purple jewel." Var., Ione, Ionia.

IONE: (Greek) "violet-colored stone." *See also* Iona.

IRENE: (Greek) "peace." Var. and dim., Eirene, Irena, Irina, Rena, Renata, Rene, Reni, Rennie, Renny.

IRIS: (Greek) "rainbow."

IRMA: (Teutonic) "strong." Var. and dim., Erma, Erme; Irmina, Irmine, Irme.

IRVETTE: (Old English) "sea friend."

ISA: (Old German) "iron-willed one."

ISABEL: (Hebrew) "consecrated to God." Originally from the name Elizabeth. Var. and dim., Isabella, Isabelle, Isbel, Isobel; Bel, Bella, Belle.

ISADORA: (Greek) "a gift." Feminine of Isidore. Var. and dim., Isidora; Dora, Dori, Dory, Issy, Izzy.

ISOLDE: (Celtic) "the fair." Var., Isolda.

ITA: (Old Irish Gaelic) "thirst."

IVAH: (Hebrew) "God's gracious gift." Var., Iva.

IVY: (origin uncertain) "a plant or a vine."

JACINDA: (Greek) "beautiful; comely." Var., Jacenta.

JACOBA: (Latin) feminine of Jacob.

JACQUELINE: (Hebrew) "the supplanter." Feminine of Jacques.

JADA: (Hebrew) "wise." Var., Jadah, Jadda.

JADE: (Spanish) "jade stone."

JAN: *see* Jane.

JANE: (Hebrew) "God's gracious gift." Feminine of John. Var. and dim., Gian, Gianna, Janet, Janette, Janice, Jayne, Jean, Jeanette, Jeanne, Jeannine, Joan, Joana, Joanna, Johanna, Juana, Juanita; Jan, Janey, Janna, Jeanie, Joanie, Jone, Jonie.

JANET, JANETTE, JANICE: *see* Jane.

JARVIA: (Old German) "spear-keen."

JASMINE: (Persian) "fragrant flower." Var., Jasmin, Jasmina, Yasmine.

JAYNE: (Sanskrit) "victorious one."

JEAN, JEANETTE, JEANNE: *see* Jane.

JEANNINE: *see* Jane.

JEMIMAH: (Hebrew) "dove." Var., Jemima, Jemmima.

JENNIE, JENNIFER, JENNY: *see* Guinevere.

JERALDINE: *see* Geraldine.

JERRI, JERRIE, JERRY: *see* Geraldine.

JESSE: *see* Jessica.

JESSICA: (Hebrew) "rich" or "grace of God." Feminine of Jesse. Dim., Jess, Jesse, Jessi, Jessie, Jessy.

JEWEL: (Latin) "a precious stone."

JILL: *see* Julia.

JINNY: *see* Virginia.

JINX: (Latin) "a charm or spell."

JO: *see* Josephine.

JOAKIMA: (Hebrew) "the Lord will set up or judge."

JOAN, JOANNA: *see* Jane.

JOBINA: (Hebrew) "the afflicted." Var., Jobyna.

JOCELYN: (Latin) "the fair." Var. and dim., Jocelin, Joslyn; Lyn, Lynn.

JOCOSA: (Latin) "humorous, joking."

JODIE: *see* Judith.

JOHANNA: *see* Jane.

JOLIE: (French) "pretty."

JORDANA: (Hebrew) "the descending." Feminine of Jordan.

JOSEPHINE: (Hebrew) "she shall add." Feminine of Joseph. Var. and dim., Josephina; Fifi, Jo, Josie.

JOVITA: (Latin) "joyful."

JOY: (Latin) "joy."

JOYCE: (Latin) "joyful."

JUANITA: *see* Jane.

JUDITH: (Hebrew) "admired; praised." Var. and dim., Juditha; Jodie, Jody, Judy.

JULIA: (Greek) "youthful." Feminine of Julius. Var. and dim., Juliana, Juliane, Juliet, Julietta, Juliette; Julie, Jill.

JULIETTE: *see* Julia.

JUNE: (Latin) "young."

JUNO: (Latin) "queen of the gods."

JUSTINE: (Latin) "the just." Feminine of Justin. Var. and dim., Justina; Tina.

K

KAMA: (Sanskrit) "love."

KAREN, KARIN, KARYN: *see* Katherine.

KARLA: *see* Carla.

KAROL: *see* Carol.

KAROLINA, KAROLINE, KAROLYN: *see* Caroline.

KASMIRA: (Old Slavic) "commands peace."

KATE: *see* Katherine.

KATHERINE: (Greek) "pure." Var. and dim., Catharine, Catherina, Catherine, Cathleen, Karen, Karena, Karin, Karyn, Katharina, Katharine, Katherin, Kathleen, Kathlene, Kathryn, Katrina; Cassie, Ina, Kara, Kate, Kathie, Kathy, Katie, Ketti, Kit, Kittie, Kitty, Trina.

KATHLEEN, KATHLENE: *see* Katherine.

KATHY: *see* Katherine.

KATRINA: *see* Katherine.

KAY: (Greek) "rejoice."

KEELY: (Irish Gaelic) "beautiful one."

KELDA: (Old Norse) "a spring."

KELLY: (Irish Gaelic) "warrior maid."

KENDRA: (Anglo-Saxon) "the knowing woman."

KERRY: (Irish Gaelic) "dark one."

KETTI: *see* Katherine.

KETURA: (Hebrew) "incense."

KEVIN: (Irish Gaelic) "gentle, lovable."

KIM: (origin uncertain) "noble" or "glorious leader."

KIMBERLY: (Old English) "from the royal fortress meadow."

KINETA: (Greek) "active one."

KIRBY: (Anglo-Saxon) "from the church town." Var., Kirbee, Kirbie.

KIRSTEN: (Scandinavian) "the anointed one."

KIT, KITTY: *see* Katherine.

KOREN: (Greek) "young girl."

KRISTIANA, KRISTINA, KRISTINE: *see* Christine.

KYLA: (Gaelic) "comely."

KYNA: (Irish Gaelic) "intelligence, wisdom."

L

LAINE: *see* Elaine.

LALA: (Slavic) "the tulip flower."

LALITA: (Sanskrit) "pleasing, artless."

LANA: *see* Alana.

LANETTE: (Old Anglo-French) "from the little lane."

LARA: (Latin) "well-known."

LARAINE: *see* Lorraine.

LARISSA: (Greek) "cheerful one."

LARK: (Middle English) "singing lark or skylark."

LA ROUX: (French) "redhead."

LASCA: (Latin) "weary; weariness."

LASSIE: (Middle English) "little girl."

LATONIA: (Latin) "sacred to Latona."

LAURA: (Latin) "the laurel." Feminine of Lawrence. Var. and dim., Laureen, Laurel, Lauren, Laurette, Lora,

Loralie, Lorelie, Loren, Loretta, Lorette, Lorinda, Lorine, Lorna, Lorne; Lari, Loree, Lori, Lorie, Lorrie.

LAUREEN, LAUREN: *see* Laura.

LAURETTE: *see* Laura.

LAVEDA: (Latin) "purified one."

LAVERNE: (French) "springlike." Var. and dim., Laverna, LaVerne; Verna, Verne, Vern.

LAVINIA: (Latin) "woman of Rome." Var. and dim., Lavina; Vina, Vinia.

LEAH: (Hebrew) "the weary." Var. and dim., Lea, Leigh; Leda, Lida.

LEANNE: (Anglo-Saxon) combination of Lee and Anne. Var., Liana, Lianne.

LEATRICE: compound of Leah and Beatrice.

LEDA: *see* Alida, Leah.

LEE: (Anglo-Saxon) "meadow." Var., Lea, Leigh.

LEILA: (Arabic) "black" or "dark as the night." Var. and dim., Leilah, Leela, Lee.

LEILANI: (Hawaiian) "Heavenly flower."

LELA, LELAH, LELIA: *see* Lillian.

LEMUELA: (Hebrew) "consecrated to God."

LENA, LINA: a dim. of Helena, Carolina, etc., but used as an independent name.

LENIS: (Latin) "smooth, soft, mild."

LENORE, LEONORA, LEONORE: *see* Helen.

LEODA: (Old German) "woman of the people."

LEOMA: (Old English) "light, brightness."

LEOLA: (Latin) a feminine form of Leo. *See also* Leona.

LEONA: (Latin) "the lion." Another feminine form of Leo. Var. and dim., Leola, Leone, Leoni, Leonie; Lee, Lennie, Lenny.

LEONARDA: (Old Frankish) "lion-brave."

LEONTINE: (Latin) "brave as a lion." Another feminine form of Leo. Var., Leontyne.

LEOPOLDINE: (Old German) "bold for the people."

LESLEY: (Celtic) "from the gray fort." Feminine of Leslie. Var. and dim., Leslie, Lesli, Lesly; Les.

41

LETA: *see* Letitia.

LETITIA: (Latin) "joy; delight." Var. and dim., Leticia; Leta, Lettie, Letty, Tish.

LETTIE, LETTY: *see* Charlotte, Letitia.

LEWANNA: (Hebrew) "the beaming, white one; the moon."

LIBBY: *see* Elizabeth.

LIDA: (Slavonic) "loved by all." Var., Lyda. *See also* Alida, Leah.

LILA, LILAH, LILLA: *see* Delilah, Lillian.

LILAC: (Persian) "bluish color; a lilac flower."

LILITH: (East Semitic) "belonging to the night."

LILLIAN: (Latin) "a lily." Var. and dim., Lela, Lelah, Lelia, Lila, Lilah, Lilia, Lilian, Lilyan; Lil, Lilla, Lilli, Lillie, Lilly, Lily.

LILLIE, LILLY, LILY: *see* Lillian.

LILLITH: (Hebrew) "evil woman; bad wife." Var., Lilith, Lilis.

LILYBELLE: (Latin) "the beautiful lily." Var., Lillibel, Lilybell, plus all dim. of Lillian.

LINDA: (Spanish) "beautiful." A dim. of Belinda, etc., but also used as an independent name. Var. and dim., Lynda; Lind, Lindie, Lindy, Lynd.

LINNEA: (Old Norse) "lime tree."

LISA, LISE, LIZ, LIZA, LIZZIE, LIZZY: *see* Elizabeth.

LISABET, LISABETH, LISBETH: *see* Elizabeth.

LIVA: *see* Olivia.

LODEMA: (Old English) "pilot or guide."

LOIS: (Greek) "battle maiden." A feminine form of Louis. *See also* Aloysia.

LOLA: (Spanish) "strong woman." A feminine form of Charles. Dim., Loleta, Lolita. *See also* Theola.

LOLITA: *see* Lola.

LORA: *see* Laura, Helen.

LORALIE: *see* Laura.

LORELEI: (Teutonic) "lurer to the rocks."

LORETTA: *see* Laura.

LORI, LORIE, LORRIE: *see* Laura.

LORINE: *see* Laura, Helen.

LORNA: *see* Laura.

LORRAINE: (Teutonic) "famous in battle." Var., Laraine, Loraine.

LOTTA, LOTTIE, LOTTY: *see* Charlotte.

LOTUS: (Egyptian) "flower of the lotus tree; bloom of forgetfulness."

LOUISE: (Teutonic) "battle maiden." Another feminine form of Louis. Var. and dim., Eloise, Heloise, Louisa; Lou, Loyce.

LOVE: (Old English) "tender affection."

LOYCE: *see* Louise.

LU, LULU: *see* Lucy.

LUANA: (Old German-Hebrew) "graceful battle maid."

LUBA: (Slavonic) "lover." Var., Lubba.

LUCILLE: *see* Lucy.

LUCRETIA: *see* Lucy.

LUCY: (Latin) "light." Feminine of Lucius. Var. and dim., Lucia; Lucilla, Lucille, Lucinda, Lucie, Lucretia; Lu, Lulu.

LUDELLA: (Old English) "famous elf."

LUDMILLA: (Old Slavic) "beloved by the people."

LUELLA: (Latin) "the appeaser." Var., Louella.

LUNA: (Latin) "of the moonlight."

LUPE: (Spanish-Mexican) "wolf."

LYDIA: (Greek) "cultured." Dim., Liddy.

LYNN: a dim. of Evelyn, Madeline, etc., but also used as an independent name. Var., Lyn, Lynna, Lynne.

LYRIS: (Greek) "of the music of the lyre; lyrical." Var., Liris.

LYSANDRA: (Greek) "liberator of men."

M

MAB: (Irish Gaelic) "mirth, joy."

MABEL: (Latin) "amiable; lovable." Var. and dim., Maybelle, Maybelle; Belle, Mae.

MADA: *see* Madeleine.

MADELINE: (Hebrew) "a tower of strength." Var. and dim., Madeleine, Madelene, Madelon, Magdalen, Marleen, Marlene, Marline; Mada, Maddie, Madid, Magda.

MADGE: *see* Margaret.

MADRA: (Latin) "mother."

MAE: *see* May.

MAGDA, MAGDALEN: *see* Madeline.

MAGGIE: *see* Margaret.

MAGNILDA: (Old German) "powerful battle maiden."

MAGNOLIA: (Anglo-Saxon) "girl of the magnolia tree."

MAHALA: (Hebrew) "tenderness."

MAIDA: (Anglo-Saxon) "maiden." Dim., Maidy.

MAISIE: *see* Margaret.

MAJESTA: (Latin) "majestic one."

MALINA: (Hebrew) "from a high tower." Var., Melina.

MALVA: (Greek) "soft, slender."

MAMIE: *see* Mary.

MANDA, MANDIE, MANDY: *see* Amanda.

MANON: *see* Mary.

MARA: *see* Damara, Mary, Samara.

MARCELLA: *see* Marcia.

MARCIA: (Latin) "of Mars." Feminine of Mark. Var. and dim., Marcella, Marsha; Marcie, Marcy.

MARGARET: (Greek) "a pearl." Var. and dim., Madge, Margaret, Margarita, Margery, Margot, Margo, Marjorie; Gredel, Greta, Gretchen, Mag, Maggie, Maisie, Marge, Margie, Meg, Peg, Peggy.

MARGERY, MARJORIE: *see* Margaret.

MARGO: *see* Margaret.

MARIA: *see* Mary.

MARIAM, MARIAN, MARION: *see* Mary.

MARIE: *see* Mary.

MARIETTA, MARIETTE, MINETTE: *see* Mary.

MARIGOLDE: (Anglo-Saxon) "like the flower marigold." Var., Marigold.

MARILYN: *see* Mary.

MARINA: (Latin) "sea maiden." Dim., Rina.

MARIS: (Latin) "sea star." Var. and dim., Marisa, Marras, Marris, Mari.

MARLA: *see* Mary.

MARLEEN, MARLENE, MARLINE: *see* Madeline.

MARMARA: (Greek) "flashing, glittering."

MARSHA: *see* Marcia.

MARTHA: (Aramaic) "the lady." Var. and dim., Marta, Martella, Marthe, Marti, Martie, Matti, Mattie.

MARTINA: (Latin) "belonging to Mars." Feminine of Martin. Var. and dim., Marteena, Martine; Marti, Teena, Tina.

MARVA: (Latin) "wonderful." Dim., Marvella.

MARVEL: (Old French) "a miracle."

MARY: (Hebrew) "bitter." Var. and dim., Mara, Mari, Maria, Mariam, Marian, Marie, Marietta, Mariette, Marilyn, Marion, Marla, Marya, Maureen, Minette, Miriam, Moira, Morene; Mamie, Manon, Mimi, Mitzi, Mitzie, Moll, Mollie, Molly, Polly.

MATHILDA: (Teutonic) "brave in battle." Var. and dim., Maud, Maude; Matti, Matty, Tilda, Tillie, Tilly.

MAUD, MAUDE: *see* Mathilda.

MAUREEN: *see* Mary.

MAURITA: (Latin) "little dark girl." Var. and dim., Marita, Mauretta; Mauri, Rita.

MAVIS: (Celtic) "songbird."

MAXINE: (Latin) "greatest." Feminine of Maximillian.

MAY: (Anglo-Saxon) "kinswoman." Var., Mae.

MEDEA: (Greek) "part goddess; sorceress."

MEG: *see* Margaret.

MEGAN: (Celtic) "the strong." Var., Meghan.

MEHETABEL: (Hebrew) "one of God's favored." Var., Mehitabel, Metabel.

MELANIE: (Greek) "darkness; clad in black." Var. and dim., Malan, Melan, Melania, Melina; Mel, Mellie, Melly.

MELBA: *see* Melvina.

MELINA: *see* Malina, Melanie.

MELISSA: (Greek) "honeybee." Var. and dim., Melisa; Lisa, Mel.

MELODY: (Greek) "song." Var. and dim., Melodie; Lodie.

MELVINA: (Celtic) "chief." Feminine of Melvin. Var. and dim., Malvina; Melba.

MENA: *see* Philomena.

MERCEDES: (Spanish) "merciful." Dim., Merci, Mercy.

MERCY: *see* Mercedes.

MEREDITH: (Celtic) "protector of the sea."

MERLE: (Latin) "the blackbird." Var., Merla, Meryl.

MERRIE: (Anglo-Saxon) "joyous; merry." Var., Meri.

MERRITT: (Anglo-Saxon) "of merit." Dim., Merri.

MERRY: (Middle English) "mirthful."

MERT, MERTA: *see* Myrtle.

MERTICE: (Old English) "famous and pleasant."

MERYL: *see* Merle.

MESSINA: (Latin) "a middle child."

META: (Latin) "ambitious."

METIS: (Greek) "wisdom; skill."

MIA: (Latin) "mine."

MICHAELA: (Hebrew) feminine of Michael.

MIGNON: (French) "dainty."

MILDRED: (Anglo-Saxon) "soft; gentle." Dim., Milli, Millie.

MILLICENT: (Teutonic) "strength." Var. and dim., Melicent, Milicent; Milli, Millie, Milly.

MILLIE, MILLY: *see* Camilla, Emily, Mildred, Millicent.

MIMI: *see* Mary.

MINA: *see* Wilhelmina.

MINERVA: (Greek) "wise." Dim., Min, Minnie, Minny.

MINNA: (Teutonic) "loving remembrance." Dim., Min, Mini, Minnie, Minny.

MINNIE, MINNY: *see* Minerva, Minna.

MIRA: (Latin) "wonderful one." *See also* Almira, Mirabel, Miranda.

MIRABEL: (Latin) "of great beauty." Var. and dim., Mirabelle; Mira, Bell, Belle.

MIRANDA: (Latin) "to be admired." Dim., Miri, Randie, Randy.

MIRIAM: *see* Mary.

MITZI: *see* Mary.

MODESTA: (Latin) "shy; unassuming." Var. and dim., Modeste; Desta, Deste.

MODESTY: (Latin) "modest one."

MOIRA: *see* Mary.

MOLLIE: *see* Mary.

MONA: (Latin) "the alone; the peaceful." *See also* Desdemona, Ramona.

MONICA: (Latin) "adviser." Var., Monique.

MORENE: *see* Mary.

MORGANA: (Old Welsh) "shore of the sea."

MORLA: (Hebrew) "chosen by the Lord."

MORNA: (Gaelic) "the tender and gentle." Var., Myrna.

MOSELLE: (Hebrew) "taken out of the water."

MURIEL: (Hebrew) "bittersweet." Var. and dim., Meriel, Murielle; Mur.

MYRA: (Latin) "the wonderful." Var., Mira.

MYRNA: *see* Morna.

MYRTLE: (Greek) "victorious crown." Var. and dim., Merta, Myrta; Mert, Myrt.

N

NADA: (Slavic) "hope."
NADIA: *see* Nadine.
NADINE: (French) "hope." Var. and dim., Nada, Nadia.
NAIRNE: (Scotch Gaelic) "from the alder-tree river."
NAN, NANCY: *see* Ann.
NANETTE, NINON: *see* Ann.
NAOMI: (Hebrew) "sweet; pleasant." Dim., Nomi.
NAPEA: (Latin) "she of the valleys."
NARDA: (origin uncertain) "joyous; gay." Var., Nara.
NATA: (Hindustani) "a rope-dancer."
NATALIE: (Latin) "child of Christmas." A feminine form of Nathan (*see* Nathaniel). Var. and dim., Natala, Natale, Natalee, Natalia, Natasha, Nathalie, Natica, Natika; Nat, Nattie, Netta, Nettie, Netty.
NATASHA: *see* Natalie.
NATHANIA: (Hebrew) Another feminine form of Nathan (*see* Nathaniel).
NATIVIDAD: (Spanish) "born at Christmas."
NEALA: (Irish Gaelic) "champion."
NEBULA: (Latin) "mist, a cloud."
NEDA: (Slavonic) "Sunday's child." Var. and dim., Neda, Nedda, Nedi.
NELDA: (Old English) "of the elder tree."
NELL, NELLIE, NELLY: *see* Cornelia, Helen.
NEOMA: (Greek) "the new moon."
NERINE: (Greek) "nymph of the sea." Var. and dim., Nereen, Nerin, Nerina.
NERISSA: (Greek) "of the sea." Var., Nerita.
NESSA, NESSIE: *see* Agnes.
NETTA, NETTIE: *see* Antonia, Natalie.
NEVA: (Spanish) "extreme whiteness; snow."

NEVADA: (Spanish) "white as snow."

NEYSA: a development of Agnes.

NICOLE: (Greek) "victory of the people." Feminine of Nicholas. Var. and dim., Nichola, Nicola, Nicolette, Nikola; Niki, Nikki.

NILA: (Latin) "the River Nile of Egypt."

NINA, NINETTE: *see* Ann.

NISSA: (Scandinavian) "a friendly elf or brownie."

NIXIE: (Old German) "a little water sprite."

NOEL: (Latin) "a Christmas child." Feminine of Noel. Var., Noella, Noelle.

NOKOMIS: (Chippewa Indian) "grandmother."

NOLA: (Celtic) "famous; well known." Feminine of Nolan.

NOLETA: (Latin) "unwilling."

NOLL, NOLLIE: *see* Olivia.

NONA: (Latin) "ninth born." Var. and dim., Nonna, Nonie.

NORA, NORAH: *see* Helen, Honora.

NORBERTA: (Old German) "brilliant heroine."

NORDICA: (German) "from the north."

NOREEN, NORINE, NORRIE: *see* Honora.

NORMA: (Latin) "the model" or "pattern." Feminine of Norman. Dim., Normi, Normie.

NORNA: (Old Norse) "a Viking goddess of fate."

NOVIA: (Latin) "young person."

NUALA: (Irish Gaelic) "fair-shouldered one."

NUMIDIA: (Latin) "a nomad."

NYDIA: (Latin) "a refuge."

NYSSA: (Greek) "starting point."

NYX: (Greek) "night."

O

OBELIA: (Greek) "a pointed pillar."

OCTAVIA: (Latin) "the eighth born." Feminine of Octavius. Dim., Tavia, Tavi.

ODELE: (Greek) "a melody." Var., Odel, Odelet, Odell.

ODELETTE: (French) "a little ode or lyric song."

ODELIA: (Teutonic) "prosperous." Var., Odella, Odile.

ODESSA: (Greek) "a long journey."

ODETTE: (French) "home-lover" or "little patriot." Var., Odet, Odetta.

OLA: (Scandinavian) "daughter" or "descendant." Feminine of Olaf.

OLGA: (Teutonic) "holy."

OLINDA: (Latin) "fragrant."

OLIVE: *see* Olivia.

OLIVIA: (Latin) "the olive." Feminine of Oliver. Var. and dim., Olive; Liva, Livi, Livia, Livvi, Noll, Nollie, Nolita, Olli, Ollie.

OLYMPIA: (Greek) "of the mountain of the gods."

OMA: (Arabic) feminine of Omar.

ONA, OONA: *see* Una.

ONDINE: *see* Undine.

OPAL: (Sanskrit) "jewel."

OPHELIA: (Greek) "wise" or "immortal." Dim., Phelia.

ORA, ORALIE, OREL: *see* Aurelia.

ORALIA: (Latin) "golden." *See also* Aurelia.

ORELA: (Latin) "a divine announcement."

ORENDA: (Iroquois Indian) "magic power."

ORIANA: (Latin) "the dawning."

ORIBEL: (Latin) "of golden beauty." Var. and dim., Orabel, Orabelle, Oribelle; Ori.

ORIOLE: (Latin) "fair; flaxen-haired." Var., Oriel.

ORLENA: (Latin) "the golden." Var., Orlene, Orlina.

ORNA: (Irish) "olive-colored."

ORPAH: (Hebrew) "a fawn."

ORVA: (Old English) "spear friend."

OTTILIE: (Teutonic) "battle heroine." Var. and dim., Otila, Ottillia; Otti, Ottie, Uta.

OZORA: (Hebrew) "strength of the Lord."

P

PAIGE: (Anglo-Saxon) "child" or "young." Var., Page.

PALLAS: (Greek) "wisdom, knowledge."

PALMA: (Latin) "a palm."

PALOMA: (Spanish) "a dove."

PAMELA: (origin uncertain) "loving, kind." Dim., Pam, Pammy.

PANDORA: (Greek) "talented, gifted." Dim., Dorie.

PANPHILA: (Greek) "the all-loving one."

PANSY: (Greek) "fragrant, flowerlike." Var., Pansie.

PANTHEA: (Greek) "of all the gods."

PARNELLA: (Old French) "little rock." Var., Pernella.

PAT: *see* Patricia.

PATIENCE: (Latin) "patient."

PATRICIA: (Latin) "of the nobility, well born." Feminine of Patrick. Var. and dim., Patrice; Pat, Patsy, Patti, Patty, Tricia, Trish.

PATSY: *see* Patricia.

PAULA: (Latin) "little." Feminine of Paul. Var. and dim., Paulette, Paulina, Pauline, Paulita; Pauli. Paulie.

PAULINE: *see* Paula.

PEACE: (Latin) "tranquillity."

51

PEARL: (Latin) "precious gem." Var. and dim., Pearle, Pearle, Perl; Perlie.

PEG, PEGGY: *see* Margaret.

PEGEEN: (Celtic) "pearl."

PELAGIA: (Greek) "from the sea."

PENELOPE: (Greek) "weaver." Dim., Pen, Pennie, Penny.

PENNY: *see* Penelope.

PENTHEA: (Greek) "mourner."

PEONY: (Greek) "flower." Var., Peonie.

PEPITA: (Spanish) "she shall add." Dim., Pepi, Peta.

PERDITA: (Latin) "lost."

PERFECTA: (Spanish) "perfect, accomplished one."

PERLE: *see* Pearl.

PERNELLA: *see* Parnella.

PERSEPHONE: (Greek) "sacred to the goddess of the underworld."

PERSIS: (Latin) "a woman from Persia."

PETRA: (Greek) "rock." A feminine form of Peter. Var. and dim., Peta, Petta; Pet, Pete.

PETRINA: (Greek) "steadfast; resolute." Another feminine form of Peter. Var. and dim., Petra, Petrine; Peti, Petie.

PETULA: (Latin) "peevish one." Var. and dim., Petulah; Pet.

PETUNIA: (Latin) "for the petunia flower."

PHEDRA: (Greek) "bright one."

PHELIA: *see* Ophelia.

PHENICE: (Hebrew) "from a palm tree." Var., Phenica, Phenicia.

PHILANA (Greek) "friend of mankind." Var., Philina, Philine, Phillane.

PHILIPPA: (Greek) "lover of horses." Feminine of Philip. Var. and dim., Philipa, Philippe; Pippa.

PHILOMENA: (Greek) "loving friend." Dim., Mena.

PHOEBE: (Greek) "the wise, shining one." Var., Phebe.

PHOENIX: (Greek) "the heron or eagle."

PHYLLIS: (Greek) "a green bough." Var. and dim., Philis, Phillis, Phylis; Phyl.

PIA: (Italian) "devout."

PIERRETTE: (French) "steady." Feminine of Pierre.

PILAR: (Spanish) "a fountain basin or pillar."

PIPER: (Old English) "a pipe player."

PLACIDA: (Latin) "gentle, peaceful one."

PLATONA: (Greek) Feminine of Plato.

POLLY: (Hebrew) "bitter." Dim., Pol, Poll, Pollie. *See also* Mary.

POMONA: (Latin) "fertile."

POPPY: (Latin) "fragrant."

PORTIA: (Latin) of uncertain meaning. Var., Porcia.

PRIMA: (Latin) "first born."

PRIMAVERA: (Spanish) "springtime."

PRIMROSE: (Latin) "the first rose." Dim., Rose, Rosie.

PRISCILLA (Latin) "the ancient; of long lineage." Var. and dim., Prisilla; Pris, Prissie, Prissy, Sil.

PROSPERA: (Latin) "favorable; suspicious."

PRUDENCE: (Latin) "the prudent; cautious." Dim., Pru, Prud, Prudi, Prudie, Prudy.

PRUNELLA: (French) "prune-colored."

PSYCHE: (Greek) "the soul."

PYRENA: (Greek) "fiery one."

PYTHIA: (Greek) "a prophet."

Q

QUEENA: (Teutonic) "a queen" or "a woman."

QUEENIE: *see* Regina.

QUENBY: (Scandinavian) "wife; womanly."

QUERIDA: (Spanish) "loved one."

QUINTA: (Latin) "the fifth child." Feminine of Quinton. Var., Quintina.

QUIRITA: (Latin) "citizen."

R

RABI: (Arabic) "spring" or "harvest."

RACHEL: (Hebrew) "naive and innocent; like a lamb." Var. and dim., Rachele, Rachelle, Rochelle; Rae, Ray, Shelley.

RADELLA: (Old English) "elfin counselor."

RADINKA: (Slavic) "active one."

RADMILLA: (Slavic) "worker for the people."

RAE, RAY: *see* Rachel.

RAISSA: (Old French) "thinker, believer."

RAMONA: (Teutonic) "protector." Feminine of Raymond. Dim., Mona, Rama.

RANA: (Sanskrit) "of royalty." Var. and dim., Rania, Rani.

RANDY: *see* Miranda.

RAPHAELA: (Hebrew) "blessed healer." Feminine of Raphael. Var., Rafaela.

REBA: *see* Rebba, Rebecca.

REBBA: (Hebrew) "the fourth born." Var., Reba, Rebah.

REBECCA: (Hebrew) "the captivator." Var. and dim., Rebekah; Becky, Reba, Riba, Riva.

REGINA: (Latin) "queenly." Var. and dim., Regan, Regine; Gina, Gine, Queenie, Reggie.

RENA, RENATA: *see* Irene.

RENEE: (French) "reborn." Var. and dim., Renata, Reni, Rennie.

RESEDA: (Latin) "the nignonette flower."

REVA: (Latin) "to regain strength."

REXANA: (Latin-English) "regally graceful."

RHEA: (Greek) "motherly."

RHODA: (Greek) "a garland of roses." Dim., Rodi, Rodie.

RHODANTHE: (Greek) "rose flower."

RHODIA: see Rose.

RIA: (Spanish) "a river mouth."

RICADONNA: (English-Italian) "ruling lady."

RICARDA: (Old English) feminine of Richard.

RICKY: dim. of Erica, Frederica, Roderica, etc.

RILLA: (Low German) "a stream or brook."

RISA: (Latin) "laughter."

RITA: (Greek) "a pearl." A dim. of Clarita, Margarita, Norita, etc., but also used as an independent name.

RIVA: see Rebecca.

ROANNA: (Latin) "sweet; gracious." Var., Roana, Roanne.

ROBERTA: (Anglo-Saxon) "of shining fame." Feminine of Robert. Var. and dim., Robina, Ruberta, Ruperta; Bobbe, Bobbi, Bobbie, Robbi, Robbie, Robi, Robin, Robina.

ROBIN, ROBINA: see Roberta.

ROCHELLE: see Rachel.

RODERICA: (Teutonic) "ruler" or "princess." Feminine of Roderick. Dim., Rica, Ricky.

ROHANA: (Hindu) "sandalwood."

ROLANDA: (Teutonic) "famed." Feminine of Roland. Dim., Ro, Rola.

ROMA: (Latin) "the wanderer" or "woman of Rome."

ROMOLA: (Latin) "lady of Rome."

RONALDA: (Teutonic) "powerful." Feminine of Ronald. Dim., Rona, Ronnie, Ronny.

RONNIE, RONNY: see Ronalda, Veronica.

ROSA: see Rose.

ROSABEL: (Latin) "beautiful rose." Var., Rosabella.

ROSALIE: see Rose.

ROSALIND: (Latin) "fair rose." Var. and dim., Rosalinde, Rosalyn, Roselyn, Roslyn; Ros, Roz.

ROSAMOND, ROSAMUND: *see* Rose.

ROSANNE: (Latin) "gracious rose." Var., Rosanna, Rosann.

ROSE: (Latin) "a rose." Var. and dim., Rhodia, Rosa, Rosalee, Rosaleen, Rosalia, Rosalie, Rosamond, Rosamund, Rosel, Rosella, Roselle, Rosena, Rosene, Rosetta, Rosette, Rosie, Rosina, Rosita, Rozalie, Rozina. *See also* Primrose.

ROSEMARIE: (Latin) "Mary's rose." Var., Rosemary.

ROSENA: *see* Rose.

ROWENA: (Celtic) "flowing white hair." Dim., Ro.

ROXANE: (Persian) "dawn." Var., Roxana, Roxanna, Roxanne; Rox, Roxie, Roxy.

ROYALE: (Old French) feminine of Roy.

RUBY: (Latin) "precious red stone." Var., Rubetta.

RUDELLE: (Old German) "famous one."

RUFINA: (Latin) feminine of Rufus.

RUTH: (Hebrew) "a beautiful friend." Dim., Ruthie.

S

SABA: (Greek) "woman of Sheba."

SABINA: (Latin) of uncertain meaning. Var. and dim., Sabine, Savina; Bina.

SABRINA: (Anglo-Saxon) "a princess." Dim., Brina.

SACHA: (Greek) "helpmate."

SADIE, SADYE: *see* Sarah.

SADIRA: (Persian) "the lotus tree."

SALENA: (Greek) "salty."

SALLIE, SALLY: *see* Sarah.

SALOME: (Hebrew) "a woman of perfection."

SALVIA: (Latin) "sage."

SAMANTHA: *see* Samuela.

SAMARA: (Hebrew) "watchful; cautious." Dim., Mara.

SAMUELA: (Hebrew) "name of God." Feminine of Samuel. Var. and dim., Samella, Samuelia; Sam, Samantha.

SANCIA: (Latin) "sacred."

SANDRA, SANDY: *see* Alexandra.

SAPPHIRE: (Greek) "beautiful jewel."

SARAH: (Hebrew) "princess." Var. and dim., Sadie, Sadye, Sara, Sarena, Sarene, Saretta, Sari, Shari, Sharon; Sadie, Sal, Sallie, Sally, Sarita.

SARETTA, SARITA: *see* Sarah.

SAXONA: (Old English) "a sexon."

SEBASTIANE: (Latin) feminine of Sebastian.

SECUNDA: (Latin) "second child."

SELENA: (Greek) "the moon." Var. and dim., Salene; Lena.

SELMA: (Celtic) "the fair." *See also* Anselma.

SEMELE: (Latin) "a single time."

SEMIRA: (Hebrew) "the height of the heavens."

SEPTIMA: (Latin) "seventh child."

SERAPHINA: (Hebrew) "burning or ardent one."

SERAPHINE: (Hebrew) "ardently religious." Var. and dim., Serafina, Sera.

SERENA: (Latin) "tranquil."

SHARON: (Hebrew) "of the land of Sharon." Var. and dim., Shara, Shari. *See also* Sarah.

SHEBA: *see* Bathsheba.

SHEILA: (Celtic) "musical." Dim., Shelley.

SHELLEY: *see* Rachel, Sheila.

SHERYL, SHERRY, SHERI: *see* Cherie, Shirley.

SHIRLEY: (Anglo-Saxon) "from the white meadow." Var. and dim., Sheryl, Shirlee, Shirlie; Sheri, Sherry, Shirl.

SIBYL: *see* Sybil.

SIDNEY, SIDONIE: *see* Sydney.

SIGFREDA: (Old German) "victorious and peaceful."
SIGNA: (Latin) "a signer."
SIGRID: (Old Norse) "victorious counselor."
SILVANA: *see* Sylvia.
SILVIA: *see* Sylvia.
SIMONE: (Hebrew) "heard by the Lord." Feminine of Simon. Var., Simonetta.
SOLITA: (Latin) "solitary."
SOLVIG: (Old German) "victorious battle maid."
SONDRA: *see* Alexandra.
SONIA, SONJA, SONYA: *see* Sophia.
SOPHIA: (Greek) "wisdom." Var. and dim., Sofia, Sonia, Sonja, Sonya; Soph, Sophey, Sophi, Sophie, Sophy.
SOPHIE: *see* Sophia.
SPRING: (Old English) "the springtime of the year."
STACEY: *see* Anastasia.
STARR: (Anglo-Saxon) "star."
STELLA: *see* Estelle.
STEPHANIE (Greek) "a crown" or "garland." Feminine of Stephen. Var. and dim., Stefanie, Stephana, Stephania, Stephenie; Stevie.
STORM: (Old English) "a tempest or storm."
SUNNY: (English) "bright, genial."
SUSAN: (Hebrew) "a lily." Var. and dim., Susana, Susanna, Susannah, Susanne, Suzanna, Suzetta; Sue, Susi, Susie, Susy, Suzie, Suzy.
SYBIL: (Greek) "the prophetess." Var. and dim., Sibel, Sibell, Sibyl, Sybyl; Sib, Sibbie, Sibby, Sibie.
SYDEL: (Hebrew) "the enchantress." Var., Sydelle.
SYDNEY: (Hebrew) "the enticer." Feminine of Sidney. Var. and dim., Sidney, Sidonia, Sidonie; Sid, Syd.
SYLVIA: (Latin) "forest maiden." Var. and dim., Silva, Silvana, Silvia; Syl, Sylvie.
SYNA: (Greek) "together."

T

TABITHA: (Aramaic) "the gazelle." Dim., Tabbie.

TACITA: (Latin) "silent."

TALITHA: (Aramaic) "maiden."

TALLULAH: a modern American name; "vivacious." Var. and dim., Tallula; Tallu.

TAMARA: (Hebrew) "the palm tree." Dim., Tama, Tammy.

TAMMY: *see* Tamara.

TANGERINE: (English) "girl from the city of Tangier."

TANIA: (Russian) "the fairy queen." Var., Tanya.

TANSY: (Middle Latin) "tenacious one."

TARA: (Celtic) "tower."

TAVIA: *see* Octavia.

TEENA: *see* Christine, Ernestine, etc.

TEMPEST: (Old French) "stormy one."

TERENTIA: (Greek) "guardian."

TERESA: (Greek) "the harvester." Var. and dim., Theresa, Therese, Tracey, Tracy; Tess, Tessa, Tessie, Zita.

TESS, TESSA, TESSIE: *see* Teresa.

THADDEA: (Greek) "courageous one."

THALIA: (Greek) "blooming."

THEA, THIA: *see* Alethea, Althea, Anthea, Theodora.

THEANO: (Greek) "divine name."

THECLA: (Greek) "divinely famous."

THEDA: *see* Theodora.

THELMA: (Greek) "nursing."

THEO: *see* Theodora, Theola.

THEODORA: (Greek) "God's divine gift." A feminine form of Theodore. Var. and dim., Theodosia; Dora, Dori, Teddi, Teddie, Theda, Thea, Theo, Thia.

THEOLA: (Greek) "heaven-sent." Dim., Lola, Theo.

THERA: (Greek) "untamed."

THERESA: *see* Teresa.

THETIS: (Greek) "positive, determined one."

THIRZA: (Hebrew) "pleasantness."

THOMASINA: (Hebrew) "the twin." Feminine of Thomas. Var., Thomasa, Thomasine.

THORA: (Teutonic) "thunder."

THORDIS: (Old Norse) "Thor-spirit."

THYRA: (Greek) "shield bearer."

TIBELDA: (Old German) "boldest of the people."

TIBERIA: (Latin) "of the River Tibes."

TILDA, TILLIE, TILLY: *see* Mathilda.

TIMOTHEA: (Greek) "honoring God." Feminine of Timothy.

TINA: dim. of Christine, Ernestine, Martina, etc., but also used as an independent name.

TIPPI, TIPPIE: *see* Zipporah.

TITA: (Latin) "a title of honor."

TITANIA: (Greek) "giant."

TOBEY: (Hebrew) "God is good." Feminine of Tobias. Var. and dim., Tobe, Tobi.

TONI: *see* Antonia.

TOPAZ: (Latin) "a topaz gem."

TOURMALINE: (Sinhalese) "a tourmaline gem."

TRACY: *see* Teresa.

TRAVIATA: (Italian) "one who goes astray."

TRICIA, TRISH: *see* Patricia.

TRILBY: (of uncertain origin) "frivolous; giddy."

TRINA: *see* Katherine.

TRISTA: (Latin) "woman of sadness."

TRIXIE: *see* Beatrice.

TRUDY: *see* Gertrude.

TSIPORAH: *see* Zipporah.

TUESDAY: (Old English) "born on Tuesday."
TULLIA: (Irish Gaelic) "peaceful, quiet one."
TZIGANE: (Hungarian) "a gypsy."

U

UDA: (Old German) "prosperous one."
UDELE: (Anglo-Saxon) "woman of great wealth."
ULA: (Celtic) "sea jewel."
ULIMA: (Arabic) "wise, learned one."
ULLAH: (Hebrew) "a burden."
ULRICA: (Teutonic) "ruler of all." Feminine of Ulric. Var. and dim., Ulrika; Rica.
ULTIMA: (Latin) "aloof one."
ULVA: (Gothic) "wolf."
UNA: (Latin) "all truth is one." Var., Ona, Oona.
UNDINE: (Latin) "of water." Var., Ondine.
URANIA: (Greek) "heavenly." Var., Uranie.
URIA: (Hebrew) "light of the Lord." Var., Uriah.
URSULA: (Latin) "she-bear." Var. and dim., Ursa, Ursel, Ursi, Ursulette.
UTA: *see* Ottilie.

V

VALA: (Gothic) "chosen one."
VALBORGA: (Old German) "protecting ruler."
VALDA: (Teutonic) "battle heroine." Dim., Val.
VALENTINA: (Latin) "the vigorous and strong." Femi-

nine of Valentine. Var. and dim., Valencia, Valentia, Valerie, Valeria, Valora; Val, Vallie.

VALERIE: *see* Valentina.

VALESKA: (Old Slavic) "glorious ruler."

VALONIA: (Latin) "from the vale."

VANESSA: (Greek) "the butterfly." Dim., Van, Vanni.

VANIA: (Hebrew) "God's gracious gift." A feminine form of John. Dim., Van.

VANORA: (Old Welsh) "white wave."

VASHTI: (Hebrew) "fairest, most lovely woman." Var., Vashta, Vasti.

VEDA: (Sanskrit) "wise."

VEGA: (Arabic) "the falling one."

VELDA: (Teutonic) "of great wisdom." Var., Valeda.

VELMA: *see* Wilhelmina.

VELVET: (Middle English) "velvety."

VEMTIRA: (Spanish) "happiness and good luck."

VENUS: (Latin) "loveliness."

VERA: (Latin) "true."

VERDA: (Latin) "young and fresh." Dim., Verdie.

VERN: *see* Laverne.

VERNA: (Latin) "spring-born." Feminine of Vernon. Var., Vernice, Vernita. *See also* Laverne.

VERONICA: (Latin) "true image." Var., Ronnie, Ronny, Vonny.

VESPERA: (Latin) "the evening star."

VESTA: (Latin) "guardian of the sacred fire" or "vestal virgin." Dim., Esta.

VEVILA: (Irish Gaelic) "melodious, harmonious lady."

VICKI, VICKY: *see* Victoria.

VICTORIA: (Latin) "the victorious." Feminine of Victor. Var. and dim., Victorie, Victorine; Vicki, Vicky.

VIDA: (Hebrew) "beloved one."

VIGILIA: (Latin) "awake and alert."

VIGNETTE: (French) "little vine."

VINNA: (Anglo-Saxon) "of the vine." Var., Vina, Vine.

VIOLA: *see* Violet.

VIOLET: (Latin) "modest; shy." Var. and dim., Viola, Violetta, Violette; Vi.

VIONA: *see* Fionna.

VIRGILIA: (Latin) "rod or staff bearer."

VIRGINIA: (Latin) "maidenly; pure." Var. and dim., Virgilia, Virginie; Ginger, Ginny, Jinny, Virg, Virgy.

VIRIDIS: (Latin) "fresh blooming, green."

VITA: (Latin) "life."

VIVIAN: (Latin) "lovely; full of life." Var. and dim., Viviane, Vivien, Vivienne; Vi, Viv, Vivi, Vivia, Vivie.

VOLANTE: (Italian) "flying one."

VOLETA: (Old French) "a flowing veil."

VONNIE, VONNY: *see* Veronica, Yvonne.

W

WALDA: (Old German) "ruler."

WALLIS: (Teutonic) "girl of Wales." Dim., Walli, Wallie, Wally.

WANDA: (Teutonic) "the wanderer." Var., Wenda.

WANETTA: (Old English) "pale one."

WARDA: (Old German) feminine of Ward.

WENDY: *see* Gwendolen.

WENONA: (American Indian) "the first born." Var. and dim., Wenonah, Winona; Winnie, Winny.

WILDA: (Anglo-Saxon) "the untamed; the wild one."

WILFREDA: (Teutonic) "firm peacemaker." Feminine of Wilfred. Dim., Freda.

WILHELMINA: (Teutonic) "protectress." Var. and dim., Velma, Wilma; Mina.

WILLA: (Anglo-Saxon) "desirable." Feminine of William.

WILMA: *see* Wilhelmina.

WINEMA: (Modoc Indian) "woman chief."

WINIFRED: (Teutonic) "friend of peace." Dim., Winnie, Winny.

WINNIE, WINNY: *see* Edwina, Wenona, Winifred.

WINONA: *see* Wenona.

WYNNE: (Celtic) "the fair" or "the white." Var., Wyne.

X

XANTHE: (Greek) "blond."

XAVIERA: (Spanish) "owner of the new house."

XENA: (Greek) "hospitable." Var., Xenia, Zenia.

XINA: *see* Christine.

XYLIA: (Greek) "of the wood."

XYLOMA: (Greek) "from the forest."

Y

YASMINE: *see* Jasmine.

YEDDA: (Old English) "to sing."

YETTA: (Teutonic) "mistress of the house."

YOLANDE: (Latin) "modest; shy." Var., Eolande, Yolanda.

YVETTE: *see* Yvonne.

YVONNE: (French) "the archer." Var. and dim., Ivonne, Yvette; Von, Vonnie.

Z

ZABRINA: (Anglo-Saxon) "of the nobility." Var. and dim., Zabrine; Brina.

ZADA: (Arabic) "lucky one."

ZANDRA: (Greek) "friend" or "helper of mankind."

ZARA: (Hebrew) "east dawn brightness."

ZEA: (Latin) "a kind of grain."

ZEBADA: (Hebrew) "gift of the Lord." Feminine of Zebadiah. Dim., Zeba.

ZELDA: *see* Griselda.

ZENA: (Greek) "hospitable." Var., Zeena, Zenia.

ZENOBIA: (Greek) "having life from Jupiter."

ZERA: (Hebrew) "seeds."

ZERLINA: (Teutonic) "serene and beautiful." Var. and dim., Zerline; Zerla.

ZETA: (Greek) the sixth letter of the Greek alphabet.

ZEVA: (Greek) "sword."

ZILLA: (Hebrew) "shadow."

ZINAH: (Hebrew) "abundance." Var., Zina.

ZINNIA: (Latin) "the zinnia flower."

ZIPPORAH: (Hebrew) "bird." Var. and dim., Ceporah, Tsiporah, Zippora; Tippi, Tippie.

ZITA: a dim. of Rosita, Theresa.

ZOE: (Greek) "life."

ZONA: (Latin) "a girdle."

ZORA: (Latin) "dawn." Var., Zorah, Zorana, Zorina.

ZULEIKA: (Arabic) "fair."

NAMES FOR

Boys

A

AARON: (Hebrew) "light; high mountain." Var., Aron.

ABBOT: (Hebrew) "father." Var., Abbott.

ABE, ABIE: *see* Abraham.

ABEL: (Hebrew) "breath."

ABELARD: (Teutonic) "resolute; ambitious."

ABNER: (Hebrew) "of light; bright." Dim., Ab, Abbie.

ABRAHAM: (Hebrew) "father of many; exalted father." Var. and dim., Abram, Avram; Abe, Abie, Bram.

ABRAM: *see* Abraham.

ABSALOM: (Hebrew) "father of peace."

ACE: (Latin) "unity."

ACKERLY: (Old English) "dweller at the acre meadow."

ACKLEY: (Old English) "dweller at the oak-tree meadow."

ADAIR: (Celtic) "from the oak-tree ford."

ADALARD, ADELARD: *see* Albert.

ADALBERT: *see* Albert.

ADAM: (Hebrew) "red earth; man of earth." Var. and dim., Adams, Adamson; Ad, Abby. *See also* Adin.

ADDISON: (Anglo-Saxon) "Adam's descendant."

ADIN: (Hebrew) "voluptuous; sensual." Var., Adam.

ADLAI: (Hebrew) "just."

ADLER: (Old German) "eagle."

ADNEY: (Old English) "dweller on the noble one's island."

ADOLPH: (Teutonic) "noble wolf." Var. and dim., Adolf, Adolphe, Adolphus; Dolph.

ADON: (Phoenician) "lord."

ADONIS: (Greek) "handsome."

ADRIAN: (Latin) "man of the seacoast." Var., Adrien, Hadrian.

ADRIEL: (Hebrew) "from God's congregation."

AENEAS: (Greek) "the praised one."

AHAB: (Hebrew) "uncle."

AHERN: (Celtic) "horse lord."

AINSLEY: (Old English) "of a nearby meadow."

ALAN: (Celtic) "harmony." Var., Alain, Allan, Allen.

ALARIC: (Teutonic) "ruler of all." Var. and dim., Alarick, Ulric, Ulrich, Ulrick; Rich, Richie, Rick, Ricky.

ALASTAIR: *see* Alexander.

ALBAN: (Latin) "white." Var., Alben, Albin, Alva.

AIDAN: (Irish Gaelic) "little fiery one."

AIKEN: (Old North English) "little Adam."

ALBERN: (Old English) "noble warrior."

ALBERT: (Teutonic) "noble and bright." Var. and dim., Adalard, Adalbert, Adelard, Albrecht, Delbert, Elbert, Ethelbert; Al, Bert, Bertie.

ALBION: *see* Aubin.

ALCOTT: (Celtic) "from the stone cottage." Var., Alcot.

ALDEN: (Anglo-Saxon) "old friend." Var. and dim., Aldin, Aldwin, Alwin; Al.

ALDO: (Teutonic) "rich."

ALDOUS: (Teutonic) "old; wise." Var., Aldis, Aldus.

ALDRICH: (Teutonic) "king."

ALDWIN: *see* Alden.

ALEC, ALEX: *see* Alexander.

ALERON: (Middle Latin) "eagle."

ALEXANDER: (Greek) "protector of men." Var. and dim., Alastair, Allister, Sanders, Sandor, Saunders; Al, Alec, Aleck, Alex, Alexis, Alick, Lex, Sandy.

ALEXIS: *see* Alexander.

ALFONSO: *see* Alphonse.

ALFORD: (Old English) "the old ford or river crossing."

ALFRED: (Anglo-Saxon) "wise as an elf." Dim., Al, Alf, Alfie, Alfy.

ALGER: (Anglo-Saxon) "spearman." Var., Algar.

ALGERNON: (French) "with whiskers." Dim., Al, Algie.

ALISON: (Old English) "noble one's son."

ALLARD: (Old English) "sacred and brave."

ALLISTER: *see* Alexander.

ALONZO: *see* Alphonse.

ALOYSIUS: *see* Lewis.

ALPHONSE: (Teutonic) "prepared for battle." Var. and dim., Alfonso, Alonzo, Alphonso; Lon, Lonny.

ALPIN: (Pictish-Scotch) "blond one."

ALROY: (Irish Gaelic) "red-haired youth."

ALSTON: (Anglo-Saxon) "from the old manor" or "village."

ALTMAN: (Old German) "old, wise man."

ALTON: (Old English) "dweller at the old town or estate."

ALVA: *see* Alban.

ALVAH: (Hebrew) "exalted one."

ALVIN: (Teutonic) "friend of all." Var., Alvan, Alwin, Alwyn, Elvin.

ALVIS: (Old Norse) "all-wise."

AMASA: (Hebrew) "burden bearer."

AMBERT: (Teutonic) "shining light; bright."

AMBROSE: (Greek) "belonging to the immortals."

AMERIGO: (Italian) explorer after whom America was named.

AMMON: (Egyptian) "the hidden."

AMORY: (Latin) "lover; loving." Var., Amary, Amery.

AMOS: (Hebrew) "a burden."

ANASTATIUS: (Greek) "one who is reborn." Var., Anastas, Anastasius.

ANATOLE: (Greek) "of the east." Var., Anatol.

ANDRE: *see* Andrew.

ANDREW: (Greek) "manly." Var. and dim., Anders, Andre, Andreas, Andrien; Andy, Drew.

ANGELO: (Greek) "saintly."

ANGUS: (Celtic) "exceptional; outstanding." Dim., Gus.

ANNAN: (Celtic) "from the stream."

ANSCOM: (Old English) "dweller in the valley of the awe-inspiring one."

ANSEL: (Old French) "adherent of a nobleman." *See also* Anselm.

ANSELM: (Teutonic) "divine helmet of God." Var., Ansel.

ANSLEY: (Old English) "from the awe-inspiring one's pasture meadow."

ANSON: (Anglo-Saxon) "the son of Ann."

ANSTICE: (Greek) "resurrected one."

ANTHONY: (Latin) "of inestimable worth." Var. and dim., Antoine, Anton, Antoni, Antonio, Antony; Tony.

ANTON, ANTONIO: *see* Anthony.

ANWELL: (Welsh-Celtic) "beloved or dear one."

ANYON: (Welsh-Celtic) "anvil."

ARCHARD: (Anglo-French-German) "sacred, powerful."

ARCHER: (Old English) "bowman." *See also* Archibald.

ARCHIBALD: (Teutonic) "truly bold." Var. and dim., Archer; Arch, Archie, Archy.

ARCHIE, ARCHY: *see* Archibald.

ARDEN: (Latin) "fervent; eager and sincere."

ARDLEY: (Old English) "from the home-lover's meadow."

ARGUS: (Greek) "watchful; vigilant." Dim., Gus.

ARGYLE: (Scotch Gaelic) "from the land of the Gaels; an Irishman."

ARIC: (Old English) "sacred ruler."

ARIES: (Latin) "a ram."

ARLEDGE: (Old English) "dweller at rabbit lake."

ARLEN: (Irish Gaelic) "pledge."

ARLIE: *see* Harley.

ARMAND, ARMIN, ARMOND: *see* Herman.

ARMSTRONG: (Old English) "with a strong arm."

ARNALL: (Old German) "eagle gracious."

ARNETT: (Old Franco-English) "little eagle."

ARNEY: (Old German) "eagle."

ARNO: (Old German) "eagle wolf."

ARNOLD: (Teutonic) "strong as an eagle." Dim., Arne, Arnie, Arno.

ARNOT: (Old Franco-German) "little eagle."

AROLPH: (Old English) "home-loving wolf."

ARTEMAS: (Greek) "gift of Artemis."

ARTHUR: (Celtic) "strong as a rock." Var. and dim., Arturo; Art, Artie.

ARTURO: *see* Arthur.

ARUNDEL: (Old English) "dweller at the eagle dell."

ARVAD: (Hebrew) "wanderer."

ARVAL: (Latin) "wept over."

ARVIN: (Teutonic) "a friend of the people." Dim., Arv, Arvie, Arvy.

ASA: (Hebrew) "healer."

ASCOT: (Old English) "dweller at the east cottage."

ASHBURN: (Old English) "ash-tree brook."

ASHBY: (Old English) "ash-tree farm."

ASHER: (Hebrew) "fortunate."

ASHFORD: (Old English) "dweller at the ash-tree ford."

ASHLEY: (Anglo-Saxon) "a dweller in the ash-tree meadow." Dim., Lee.

ASHLIN: (Old English) "dweller at the ash-tree pool."

ASHTON: (Old English) "dweller at the ash-tree farm."

ASHUR: (East Semitic) "warlike one."

ASWIN: (Old English) "spear-friend or protector."

ATHERTON: (Old English) "dweller at the spring farm."

ATLEY: (Old English) "dweller at the meadow."

ATWATER: (Old English) "dweller at the water."

ATWELL: (Old English) "dweller at the spring."

ATWOOD: (Old English) "dweller at the forest."

ATWORTH: (Old English) "dweller at the farmstead."

AUBIN: (Latin) "fair; white." Var., Albion.

AUBREY: (Teutonic) "elf-ruler." Dim., Bree, Brey.

AUGUST: (Latin) "exalted." Var. and dim., Augustin, Augustine, Augustus, Austen, Austin, Gustane, Gustin; Augie, Gus.

AUGUSTINE: (Latin) "belonging to Augustus."

AURICK: *see* Warrick.

AUSTEN, AUSTIN: *see* August.

AVENALL: (Old French) "dweller at the oat field."

AVERILL: (Anglo-Saxon) "boarlike" or "of April." Var. and dim., Averil; Av.

AVERY: (Anglo-Saxon) "ruler of the elves."

AVRAM: *see* Abraham.

AXEL: (Hebrew) "man of peace." Var., Aksel.

AXTON: (Old English) "sword wielder's stone."

AYLMER: *see* Elmer.

AYLWARD: (Old English) "awe-inspiring guardian."

AYLWORTH: (Old English) "awe-inspiring one's farmstead."

B

BAILEY: (Teutonic) "able."

BAINBRIDGE: (Old English) "bridge over white water."

BAIRD: (Celtic) "the minstrel." Var., Bard.

BALBO: (Latin) "the indistinct speaker."

BALDEMAR: (Old German) "bold or princely, and famous."

BALDER: (Old English) "bold army."

BALDRIC: (Old German) "bold or princely ruler."

BALDWIN: (Teutonic) "bold, noble friend."

BALFOUR: (Pictish-Gaelic) "from the pasture place."

BALLARD: (Old German) "bold, strong."

BALTHASAR: (Greek) "may the Lord protect the king."

BANCROFT: (Anglo-Saxon) "from the bean field."

BANNING: (Irish Gaelic) "little blond one."

BARCLAY: *see* Berkeley.

BARD: *see* Baird.

BARDO: *see* Bartholomew.

BARDOLF: (Old English) "axe-wolf."

BARDRICK: (Old English) "axe ruler."

BARLOW: (Old English) "dweller at the bare hill."

BARNABY: (Hebrew) "son of consolation." Var. and dim., Barnabas; Barney.

BARNARD, BARNET, BARNETT: *see* Bernard.

BARNETT: (Old English) "nobleman; leader."

BARNEY: *see* Barnaby, Baruch, Bernard.

BARNUM: (Old English) "nobleman's home."

BARON: (Teutonic) "of noble blood." Var., Barron.

BARR: (Old English) "a gateway."

BARRET: (Teutonic) "mighty as a bear." Var., Barrett.

BARRIS: (Old Welsh) "son of Harry."

BARRY: (Celtic) "spear." *See also* Baruch.

BART, BARTH: *see* Barton, Bartholomew.

BARTHOLOMEW: (Hebrew) "son of the furrows; a plowman," Var. and dim., Bardo, Barth, Barthol, Bartholemew, Bartholemy, Bartlett, Bartley; Bart, Bat.

BARTLETT: *see* Bartholomew.

BARTLEY: (Old English) "Bart's meadow." *See also* Bartholomew.

BARTON: (Anglo-Saxon) "farmer." Dim., Bart, Barth.

BARTRAM: *see* Bertram.

BARUCH: (Hebrew) "blessed." Dim., Barney, Barrie, Barry.

BASIL: (Greek) "kingly."

BAXTER: (Teutonic) "the baker." Dim., Bax.

BAYARD: (French) "of the fiery hair."

BAYNARD: *see* Bernard.

BEACHER: (Old English) "dweller by the beech tree." Var., Beecher.

BEAGAN: (Irish Gaelic) "little one."

BEAL: (Old French) "handsome one."

BEAMAN: (Old English) "beekeeper."

BEAMER: (Old English) "trumpeter."

BEATTIE: (Irish Gaelic) "public victualer."

BEAU: (Old French) "handsome one."

BEAUFORT: (Old French) "from the beautiful stronghold."

BEAUMONT: (Old French) "from the beautiful mountain."

BECK: (Middle English) "a brook."

BEECHER: *see* Beecher.

BELDEN: (Old English) "dweller in the beautiful glen."

BELLAMY: (Old French) "handsome friend."

BEN, BENNY: *see* Benedict, Benjamin, Benton.

BENEDICT: (Latin) "bless." Var. and dim., Benedic, Benedick, Benedix, Bennet, Bennett; Ben, Benny, Dixon.

BENJAMIN: (Hebrew) "son of my right hand." Var. and dim., Benson; Ben, Benjie, Benjy, Bennie, Benny.

BENNETT: *see* Benedict.

BENSON: *see* Benjamin.

BENTLEY: (Old English) "from the bent-grass meadow."

BENTON: (Anglo-Saxon) "of the moors." Dim., Ben.

BERESFORD: (Old English) "from the barley ford."

BERG: (German) "from the mountain." *See also* Burgess.

BERGER: (French) "shepherd." *See also* Burgess.

BERKELEY: (Anglo-Saxon) "from the birch meadow." Var., Barclay, Berkley.

BERNARD: (Teutonic) "grim bear." Var. and dim., Barnard, Barnet, Barnett, Baynard, Bernarr, Bernhard; Barney, Bern, Bernie.

BERNHARD: *see* Bernard.

BERT: *see* Albert, Bertram, Burton, Egbert, Herbert, etc.

BERTHOLD: (Old German) "brilliant ruler."

BERTON: *see* Burton.

76

BERTRAM: (Latin) "bright raven." Var. and dim., Bartram, Bertrand; Bert.

BERTRAND: *see* Bertram.

BEVAN: (Celtic) "son of Evan." Var., Bevin.

BEVERLEY: (Anglo-Saxon) "from the beaver meadow."

BEVIS: (Old French) "fair view."

BICKFORD: (Old English) "hewer's ford."

BILL: *see* William.

BING: (Old German) "from the kettle-shaped hollow."

BIRCH: (Old English) "at the birch tree."

BIRKETT: (Middle English) "dweller at the birch headland."

BIRKEY: (North English) "from the birch-tree island."

BIRLEY: (Old English) "cattle shed on the meadow."

BIRNEY: (Old English) "dweller on the brook island."

BIRTLE: (Old English) "from the bird hill."

BISHOP: (Old English) "the bishop."

BLACK: (Old English) "dark-complected."

BLADE: (Old English) "prosperity, glory."

BLAGDEN: (Old English) "from the dark valley."

BLAINE: (Irish Gaelic) "thin, lean." Var., Blane, Blayne.

BLAIR: (Celtic) "a place."

BLAISE: *see* Blaze.

BLAKE: (Old English) "fair-haired and fair-complexioned."

BLAKELEY: (Old English) "from the black meadow."

BLAKEY: (Old English) "little fair-haired one."

BLANCO: (Spanish) "blond, white."

BLAND: (Latin) "mild, gentle one."

BLANE: *see* Blaine.

BLANFORD: (Old English) "Gray-haired one's river crossing."

BLASE: *see* Blaze.

BLAYNE: *see* Blaine.

BLAZE: (Latin) "stammerer." Var., Blaise, Blase.

BLISS: (Old English) "joyful one."

BLYTHE: (Old English) "merry one."

BOAZ: (Hebrew) "strength is in the lord."

BOB: *see* Robert.

BODEN: (Old French) "herald, messenger."

BOGART: (Old German) "bow-strong."

BONAR: (Old French) "kind, gentle."

BONIFACE: (Latin) "doer of good."

BOONE: (Old French) "good one."

BOOTH: (Teutonic) "from a market" or "home-lover."

BORDEN: (Old English) "he lives near the boar's den."
Var., Barden.

BORG: (Norse) "castle dweller."

BORIS: (Slavic) "a fighter."

BOSWELL: (Old French) "forest town."

BOSWORTH: (Old English) "at the cattle enclosure."

BOTOLF: (Old English) "herald wolf."

BOURNE: (Old English) "from the brook."

BOWEN: (Celtic) "the son" or "descendant of Owen."

BOWIE: (Irish Gaelic) "yellow-haired."

BOYCE: (Old French) "from the forest."

BOYD: (celtic) "light-haired."

BOYNE: (Irish Gaelic) "white cow."

BRAD: dim. of Bradford, Bradley, but also used as an
independent name.

BRADBURN: (Old English) "broad brook."

BRADEN: (Old English) "from the wide valley."

BRADFORD: (Anglo-Saxon) "from the broad ford."
Dim., Brad, Ford.

BRADLEY: (Anglo-Saxon) "from the broad meadow."
Dim., Brad.

BRADY: (Irish Gaelic) "spirited one."

BRAINARD: (Old English) "bold raven."

BRAM: *see* Abraham, Bramwell.

BRAMWELL: (Old English) "of Abraham's well." Dim.,
Bram.

BRANDON: *see* Brendan.

BRAND: (Old English) "firebrand."

BRANDER: (Old Norse) "sword; firebrand."

BRANT: (Teutonic) "fiery."

BRAWLEY: (Old English) "from the hill-slope meadow."

BRENDAN: (Celtic) "from the fiery hill." Var., Brandon, Brendon, Brennan.

BRENT: (Old English) "steep hill."

BRETT: (French) "a native of Brittany." Var., Bret.

BREWSTER: (Old English) "brewer."

BRIAN: (Celtic) "strong; powerful." Var., Bryan, Bryant.

BRICE: (Celtic) "ambitious; alert." Var., Bryce.

BRIDGER: (Old English) "bridge builder."

BRIGHAM: (Anglo-Saxon) "a dweller by the bridge."

BROCK: (Celtic) "badger."

BROCKLEY: (Old English) "from the badger meadow."

BRODIE: (Irish Gaelic) "a ditch."

BROMLEY: (Old English) "a dweller in the meadow." Var. and dim., Bromlea, Bromleigh; Brom.

BRODERICK: *see* Roderick.

BRONSON: (Old English) "son of the brown one."

BROOK: (Middle English) "dweller at the brook."

BROOKS: (Middle English) "dweller where brooks merge."

BROUGHER: (Old English) "fortress resident."

BROUGHTON: (Old English) "from the fortress town."

BROWN: (Middle English) "dark, reddish complexion."

BRUCE: (French) "from the brushwood thicket."

BRUNO: (Teutonic) "brown."

BRYAN, BRYANT: *see* Brian.

BRYCE: *see* Brice.

BUCKLEY: (Old English) "dweller at the buck deer meadow."

BUDD: (Gaelic) "winner." Var. and dim., Bud; Buddy.

BUNDY: (Old English) "free man."

BURBANK: (Old English) "dweller on the castle hill slope."

BURCH: (Middle English) "birch tree."

BURCHARD: (Old English) "strong as a castle."

BURDETT: (Old French) "little shield."

BURDON: (Old English "dweller at the castle hill."

BURFORD: (Old English) "dweller at the castle ford."

BURGESS: (Teutonic) "a townsman." Var. and dim., Berger, Bergess; Berg, Burg.

BURKE: (Teutonic) "from the stronghold" or "castle."

BURL: (Old English) "cup bearer."

BURLEY: (Old English) "dweller at the castle meadow."

BURNABY: (Old Norse) "warrior's estate."

BURNE: (Old English) "brook."

BURNELL: (Old English) "little brown-haired one."

BURNETT: (Middle English) "little brown-complected one."

BURNEY: (Old English) "dweller at the brook island."

BURR: (Old Norse) "youth."

BURRELL: (Old French) "reddish-brown complexion."

BURT: *see* Burton.

BURTON: (Anglo-Saxon) "of bright fame." Var. and dim., Berton; Bert, Burt.

BUSBY: (Scotch-Norse) "dweller at the village in the thicket."

BYFORD: (Old English) "dweller at the river crossing."

BYRAM: (Old English) "dweller at the cattle-shed place."

BYRD: (Old English) "birdlike."

BYRON: (French) "from the cottage" or "the bear."

C

CADBY: (Old Norse-English) "warrior's settlement."

CADDOCK: (Old Welsh) "battle keenness."

CADELL: (Old Welsh) "battle spirit."

CADMAN: (Celtic) "brave warrior."

CADMUS: (Greek) "man from the east."

CAESAR: (Latin) "born with long hair; leader."

CAIN: (Hebrew) "possession or possessed."

CAL: *see* Caleb, Calvin.

CALDER: (Celtic) "from the river of stones."

CALDWELL: (Old English) "cold spring."

CALEB: (Hebrew) "bold; impetuous." Dim., Cal.

CALEY: (Irish Gaelic) "thin, slender."

CALHOUN: (Irish Gaelic) "from the narrow forest."

CALVERT: *see* Calvin.

CALVIN: (Latin) "bald." Var. and dim., Calvert; Cal.

CAMDEN: (Anglo-Gaelic) "from the winding valley."

CAMERON: (Celtic) "bent nose." Dim., Cam, Camm.

CAMPBELL: (French) "from a bright field." Var., Campball.

CANUTE: (Old Norse) "knot."

CAREW: (Celtic) "from this fortress." Dim., Carr.

CAREY, CARY: *see* Charles.

CARL, CARLO, CARLOS, CARROL: *see* Charles.

CARLETON: (Old English) "farmer's settlement." *See also* Charlton.

CARLIN: (Old Irish Gaelic) "little champion."

CARLISLE: (Latin) "from a walled city; island."

CARMICHAEL: (Scotch Gaelic) "friend of St. Michael."

CARNEY: (Irish Gaelic) "victorious."

CAROLLAN: (Irish Gaelic) "little champion."

CARR: (Old Norse) "dweller at a marsh." *See also* Carew.

CARRICK: (Irish Gaelic) "rocky headland."

CARROLL: (Irish Gaelic) "champion."

CARSON: (Welsh) "his father lives near marshes."

CARSWELL: (Old English) "dweller at the watercress spring."

CARTER: (Anglo-Saxon) "cartmaker."

CARTLAND: (Scotch-English) "land between the streams."

CARVELL: (Old French) "spearman's estate."

CARVER: (Anglo-Saxon) "one who carves."

CARVEY: (Irish Gaelic) "athlete."

CARY: (Old Welsh) "dweller at the castles."

CASH: (Latin) "vain one."

CASIMIR: (Slavic) "proclamation of peace." Var. and dim., Casper, Kazimir; Cass, Cassie, Cassy.

CASPER, CASS, CASSIE: *see* Casimir, Jasper.

CASSIDY: (Irish Gaelic) "clever one."

CASTOR: (Greek) "beaver."

CATHMOR: (Irish Gaelic) "great warrior."

CATO: (Latin) "wise one."

CAVAN: (Irish Gaelic) "handsome one." Var., Kavan.

CAVELL: (Old French) "little active one."

CAWLEY: (Scotch-Norse) "ancestral relic."

CECIL: (Latin) "blind."

CEDRIC: (Celtic) "chieftain."

CHAD: (Old English) "warlike."

CHADWICK: (Celtic) "defender." Dim., Chad.

CHALMER: (Teutonic) "king of the household."

CHANCE: (Middle English) "good fortune."

CHANCELOR: *see* Chauncey.

CHANDLER: (French) "candlemaker." Dim., Chan.

CHANNING: (Anglo-Saxon) "a regent; knowing."

CHAPIN: (French) "a man of God." Var., Chapen, Chapland, Chaplin.

CHARLES: (Teutonic) "man." Var. and dim., Carey, Carl, Carol, Carrol, Karl, Karol; Carlo, Carlos, Cary, Charley, Charlie, Chas, Chuck.

CHARLTON: (Anglo-Saxon) "of Charles' farm." Var., Carleton, Carlton, Charleton.

CHASE: (Old French) "hunter."

CHATHAM: (Old English) "soldier's land."

CHAUNCEY: (French) "official record keeper." Var., Chancelor, Chancellor.

CHENEY: (Old French) "dweller at the oak forest."

CHESTER: (Latin) "of the fortified camp." Var. and dim., Cheston; Chet.

CHET: *see* Chester.

CHETWIN: (Old English) "from the cottage on the winding path."

CHILTON: (Anglo-Saxon) "from the farm by the spring." Var., Chelton.

CHRISTIAN: (Latin) "a Christian." Var. and dim., Kristian, Kristin; Chris, Kit.

CHRISTOPHER: (Greek) "Christ-bearer." Dim., Chris, Christie, Christy, Kester, Kit, Kris, Kriss.

CHUCK: see Charles.

CHURCHILL: (Old English) "dweller at the church hill."

CIAN: (Irish Gaelic) "ancient."

CICERO: (Latin) "chick-pea."

CLAIR: (Latin) "famous one." See also Clarence.

CLARENCE: (Anglo-Saxon) "bright; illustrious." Dim., Clari, Clair, Cole.

CLARK: (Latin) "scholarly; wise." Var., Clarke.

CLAUD: (Latin) "lame." Var. and dim., Claude; Claudy.

CLAUS: see Nicholas.

CLAY: see Clayton.

CLAYTON: (Anglo-Saxon) "mortal man." Var. and dim., Clayborn, Clayborne; Clay.

CLEARY: (Irish Gaelic) "scholar."

CLEM: see Clement.

CLEMENT: (Latin) "mild; kind; merciful." Var. and dim., Clemence; Clem.

CLEVE: see Clive.

CLEVELAND: (Old English) "from the cliff land."

CLIFFORD: (Anglo-Saxon) "from the ford near the cliff." Dim., Cliff.

CLIFTON: (Anglo-Saxon) "from the farm at the cliff."

CLINTON: (Anglo-Saxon) "from the headland farm."

CLIVE: (Anglo-Saxon) "cliff." Var., Cleve.

CLOVIS: see Lewis.

CLUNY: (Irish Gaelic) "from the meadow."

CLYDE: (Celtic) "heard from a distance."

COBB: a dim. of Jacob.

COLAN: see Colin.

COLBERT: (Old English) "brilliant seafarer."

COLBY: (Old English) "from the dark farm."

COLE: *see* Clarence, Coleman, Colin.

COLEMAN: (Celtic) "dove keeper." Var. and dim., Colman; Col, Cole.

COLIN: (Celtic) "strong; young and virile." Var. and dim., Colan, Cole. *See also* Nicholas.

COLLEY: *see* Nicholas.

COLLIER: (Old English) "miner."

COLTER: (Old English) "colt herder."

COLTON: (Old English) "from the dark estate."

COLVER: *see* Culver.

CONAL: (Celtic) "high and mighty." Var. and dim., Conall, Conana, Conant, Connel, Kynan, Quinn; Con, Conn.

CONAN: (Celtic) "intelligence." *See also* Conal.

CONANT: *see* Conal.

CONLAN: (Irish Gaelic) "hero."

CONRAD: (Teutonic) "brave counsel." Var. and dim., Konrad; Con, Connie, Curt.

CONROY: (Celtic) "wise."

CONSTANTINE: (Latin) "unwavering; firm." Var. and dim., Constant; Conn.

CONWAY: (Celtic) "a man of the great plains."

COOPER: (Old English) "barrel maker."

CORBETT: (Old French) "raven."

CORBIN: (Latin) "the raven." Var. and dim., Corwin; Corby.

CORCORAN: (Irish Gaelic) "reddish complexion."

CORDELL: (French) "binding cord" or "rope."

COREY: (Celtic) "ravine dweller." Var., Cory.

CORMICK: (Irish Gaelic) "charioteer."

CORNELIUS: (Latin) "battle horn." Dim., Cornel, Cornell, Neal, Neil, Nelson.

CORNELL: (Old French) "horn-colored hair." *See also* Cornelius.

CORT: *see* Courtenay.

CORWIN: *see* Corbin.

CORYDON: (Greek) "crested one."

COSMO: (Greek) "universe" or "in good order."

COURTENAY: (French) "a place." Var. and dim., Court, Courtland, Courtney; Cort, Cortie, Corty.

COVELL: (Old English) "dweller at the cave slope."

COWAN: (Irish Gaelic) "hillside valley."

COYLE: (Irish Gaelic) "battle follower."

CRADDOCK: (Old Welsh) "abounding in love."

CRAIG: (Celtic) "of the crag" or "stony hill."

CRANDALL: (Old English) "of the valley of the cranes; caretaker of the cranes."

CRANLEY: (Old English) "from the crane meadow."

CRANSTON: (Old English) "from the crane town."

CRAWFORD: (Old English) "of the crow's crossing."

CREIGHTON: (Middle English) "dweller at the creek town."

CRISPIN: (Latin) "curly-haired." Var., Crispen.

CROMWELL: (Old English) "dweller at the winding stream."

CROSBY: (Anglo-Saxon) "near the crossroad."

CROSLEY: (Old English) "from the cross meadow."

CULBERT: (Teutonic) "noted and bright." Var., Colbert, Cuthbert.

CULLEN: (Irish Gaelic) "handsome one."

CULLEY: (Irish Gaelic) "at the woodland."

CULVER: (Anglo-Saxon) "gentle; peaceful; dove." Var., Colver.

CURRAN: (origin uncertain) "heroic; resolute."

CURT: *see* Conrad, Curtis.

CURTIS: (French) "courteous." Dim., Curt, Kurt.

CUTHBERT: *see* Culbert.

CUTLER: (Old English) "the knife maker."

CYNRIC: (Old English) "powerful and royal."

CYPRIAN: (Greek) "man from Cyprus."

CYRANO: (Greek) "from Cyrene."
CYRIL: (Greek) "lord."
CYRUS: (Persian) "throne." Dim., Cy, Russ.

D

DACEY: (Irish Gaelic) "southerner."
DAG: (Old Norse) "day or brightness."
DAGAN: (East Semitic) "the earth" or "little fish."
DAGWOOD: (Old English) "bright one's forest."
DALBERT: (Old English) "proud, brilliant one."
DALE: (Teutonic) "valley dweller." Var., Dalton.
DALLAS: (Celtic) "skilled" or "spirited." Dim., Dal.
DALTON: (Old English) "from the valley town." *See also* Dale.
DALY: (Irish Gaelic) "counselor."
DALZIEL: (Scotch Gaelic) "from the little field."
DAMON: (Greek) "tame; domesticated." Var., Damian.
DANA: (Scandinavian) "a Dane." Var., Dane.
DANBY: (Old Norse) "from the Dane's settlement." *See also* Denby.
DANIEL: (Hebrew) "the Lord is judge." Var. and dim., Daniell, Darnell; Dan, Danny.
DANTE: *see* Durand.
DARBY: (Irish Gaelic) "free man."
DARCY: (French) "from the stronghold." Var., D'Arcy.
DARIUS: (Persian) "a man of many possessions." Var. and dim., Darian, Derian; Darren.
DARRELL: (Anglo-Saxon) "beloved." Var. and dim., Darryl; Darren.
DARREN: dim. of Darius, Darrell, Dorian, etc., but also used as an independent name.
DARTON: (Old English) "deer park."

DAVID: (Hebrew) "beloved." Var. and dim., Davis; Dave, Davie, Davy, Dewey.

DAVIN: (Scandinavian) "the bright man; bright Finn."

DAVIS: (Old English) "son of the beloved one." *See also* David.

DEAN: (Anglo-Saxon) "valley." Var., Deane.

DEARBORN: (Anglo-Saxon) "beloved baby" or "child."

DEDRICK: (Old German) "ruler of the people."

DEEMS: (Old English) "son of the judge."

DELANO: (Old French) "from the place of the nut trees."

DELBERT: *see* Albert.

DELLING: (Old Norse) "very shining one."

DELMAR: (Latin) "of the sea." Var., Delmer.

DELWYN: (Old English) "proud friend."

DEMAS: (Greek) "popular one."

DEMETRIUS: (Greek) "lover of the earth." Var. and dim., Dimitri, Dmitri; Demmy.

DEMOS: (Greek) "the people."

DEMPSEY: (Irish Gaelic) "proud one." *See also* Dempster.

DEMPSTER: (Old English) "a judge; wise." Var. and dim., Dempstor; Dempsey.

DENBY: (Scandinavian) "from the Danish settlement; loyal Dane." Var., Danby.

DENLEY: (Old English) "dweller in the valley meadow."

DENMAN: (Old English) "valley resident."

DENNIS: (Greek) "lover of fine wines." Var. and dim., Denis, Dennison, Denys, Denzil, Dion; Dennie, Denny, Deny.

DENNISON: *see* Dennis.

DENTON: (Old English) "from the valley estate."

DENVER: (Old English) "dweller at the valley edge."

DEREK, DERRICK, DERK: *see* Theodoric.

DERMOT: *see* Kermit.

DERWARD: (Old English) "deer warden."

DERWIN: (Old English) "beloved friend."

DESMOND: (Celtic) "worldly; sophisticated." Dim., Desi.

DEVERELL: (Old Welsh-English) "from the riverbank."

DEVIN: (Celtic) "a poet."

DEVLIN: (Irish Gaelic) "fierce valor."

DEWEY: see David.

DE WITT: (Old Flemish) "blond one."

DEXTER: (Latin) "right-handed; dexterous."

DIAMOND: (Old English) "bright protector."

DICK: see Richard.

DIEGO: see James.

DIGBY: (Old Norse) "from the dike settlement."

DILLON: (Celtic) "faithful."

DION: see Dennis.

DIXON: see Benedict.

DOANE: (Celtic) "dweller of the sand dune."

DOLAN: (Irish Gaelic) "black-haired."

DOLPH: see Adolph, Rudolph.

DOMINIC: (Latin) "the Lord's." Var. and dim., Dominick; Dom, Dominy, Nic, Nick, Nicky.

DONALD: (Celtic) "ruler of the world." Var. and dim., Donal, Donall, Donnell; Don, Donn, Donnie, Donny.

DONATO: (Latin) "a gift."

DOOLEY: (Irish Gaelic) "dark hero."

DORAN: (Greek) "the stranger." Var., Dorran.

DORIAN: (Greek) "from the town of Dori." Dim., Darren, Dore, Dorey, Dory. See also Isidore.

DORY: (French) "golden-haired." See also Dorian, Isidore.

DOUGLAS: (Celtic) "from the black stream." Dim., Doug.

DOW: (Irish Gaelic) "black-haired."

DOYLE: (Celtic) "the dark stranger; newcomer."

DRAKE: (Middle English) "owner of the Dragon Inn sign."

DREW: (Teutonic) "skilled; honest." Var., Dru, Drue. See also Andrew.

DRISCOLL: (Celtic) "the speaker or interpreter."
DRUCE: (Celtic) "wise man; capable and adept."
DRURY: (Old French) "sweetheart."
DUANE: (Celtic) "singing." Var., Dwane, Dwayne.
DUDLEY: (Anglo-Saxon) "a place." Dim., Dud, Lee.
DUFF: (Irish Gaelic) "dark-complexioned one."
DUGAN: (Irish Gaelic) "dark-complexioned."
DUKE: (Latin) "leader."
DUNCAN: (Celtic) "warrior of dark skin." Dim., Dunc.
DUNLEY: (Old English) "from the hill meadow."
DUNMORE: (Scotch Gaelic) "great hill fortress."
DUNN: (Old English) "dark-complexioned one."
DUNSTAN: (Anglo-Saxon) "from the brown stone hill."
DUNTON: (Old English) "of the farm over the hill."
DURAND: (Latin) "enduring." Var., Dante, Durant.
DURWARD: (Anglo-Saxon) "the doorkeeper." Var., Durware, Durwood, Derwood.
DURWIN: (Anglo-Saxon) "dear friend." Var., Durwyn.
DUSTIN: (Teutonic) "strong-hearted leader."
DUTCH: (German) "the German."
DWAYNE: *see* Duane.
DWIGHT: (Teutonic) "light."
DYLAN: (Old Welsh) "from the sea."

E

EACHAN: (Irish Gaelic) "little horse."
EARL: (Anglo-Saxon) "nobleman; chief." Var., Earle, Early, Erle, Errol.
EATON: (Anglo-Saxon) "of the river" or "riverside."
EBEN: (Hebrew) "stone."
EBENEZER: (Hebrew) "stone of help." Dim., Eb.
EBERHART: *see* Everard.

EDAN: (Celtic) "flame."

EDBERT: (Old English) "prosperous, brilliant."

EDEL: (Old German) "noble one."

EDELMAR: (Old English) "noble, famous."

EDEN: (Hebrew) "place of delight and pleasure."

EDGAR: (Anglo-Saxon) "lucky spear; fortunate warrior." Dim., Ed, Eddie.

EDLIN: *see* Edwin.

EDMUND: (Anglo-Saxon) "fortunate" or "rich protector." Var. and dim., Edmond; Ed, Eddie, Ned, Neddy.

EDOLF: (Old English) "prosperous wolf."

EDRIC: (Anglo-Saxon) "rich ruler." Var., Edrick.

EDSEL: (Anglo-Saxon) "profound; deep thinker."

EDSON: (Anglo-Saxon) "the son of Ed." Var., Edison.

EDWALD: (Old English) "prosperous ruler."

EDWARD: (Anglo-Saxon) "prosperous guardian." Var. and dim., Eduard; Ed, Eddie, Eddy, Ned, Neddy, Ted, Teddy.

EDWIN: (Anglo-Saxon) "wealthy friend." Var. and dim., Edlin; Ed, Eddie, Eddy.

EFREM: *see* Ephraim.

EGAN: (Teutonic) "formidable." Var., Egon.

EGBERT: (Anglo-Saxon) "bright and shining sword." Dim., Bert, Bertie.

EHREN: (Old German) "honorable one."

EINAR: (Old Norse) "warrior leader."

ELBERT: *see* Albert.

ELDON: (Teutonic) "respected; older." Var. and dim., Elden; El.

ELDRIDGE: (Teutonic) "wise adviser." Var., Eldred, Eldrid.

ELDWIN: (Anglo-Saxon) "wise friend; adviser." Var., Eldwen.

ELEAZAR: (Hebrew) "helped by God." Var., Eliezer, Lazarus, Lazar.

ELEPH: (Hebrew) "strong as an ox."

ELI: (Hebrew) "the highest." Var., Elia, Ely.

ELIAS: (Hebrew) "the Lord is God." Var., Elihu, Elijah, Eliot, Elliot, Ellis.

ELIHU: (Hebrew) "God, the Lord." *See also* Elias.

ELISHA: (Hebrew) "God, my salvation."

ELLARD: (Teutonic) "nobly brave."

ELLERY: (Teutonic) "of the alder trees." Var., Elery.

ELLIOT, ELLIS: *see* Elias.

ELLISON: (Hebrew) "son of Elias." Var., Elison.

ELLSWORTH: (Anglo-Saxon) "lover of the earth; farmer." Var., Elsworth.

ELMER: (Anglo-Saxon) "noble; famous." Var., Aylmer.

ELMO: (Greek) "friendly."

ELMORE: (Old English) "dweller at the elm-tree moor."

ELROY: (Latin) "royal." Var. and dim., Leroy; Roy.

ELSDON: (Old English) "noble one's hill."

ELSTON: (Old English) "noble one's town."

ELSWORTH: (Old English) "noble one's estate." *See also* Ellsworth.

ELTON: (Anglo-Saxon) "from the old farm" or "village."

ELVIN: *see* Alvin.

ELVIS: (Old Norse) "all-wise."

ELVY: (Old English) "elfin warrior."

ELWELL: (Old English) "from the old spring."

ELWIN: (Anglo-Saxon) "a friend of elves." Var. and dim., Elwyn; Winn, Wynn.

ELWOOD: (Old English) "from the old forest."

EMERSON: (Old English) "a son of Emory."

EMIL: (Teutonic) "industrious." Var., Emlyn.

EMMANUEL: (Hebrew) "God is with us." Var. and dim., Immanuel, Manuel; Manny.

EMMET: (Anglo-Saxon) "ant; industrious." Var. and dim., Emmett; Em, Emmy.

EMORY: (Teutonic) "work leader; ambitious." Var., Emery, Merrick.

ENNIS: (Irish Gaelic) "one choice."

ENOCH: (Hebrew) "devoted."

ENOS: (Hebrew) "mortal."

ENRICO: *see* Henry.

EPHRAIM: (Hebrew) "abounding in fruitfulness." Var. and dim., Efrem; Eph.

ERASMUS: (Greek) "kindly."

ERASTUS: (Greek) "beloved."

ERIC: (Teutonic) "kingly." Var. and dim., Erich, Erick, Erik; Rick, Ricky.

ERLAND: (Teutonic) "noble eagle."

ERLE: *see* Earl.

ERLING: (Old English) "nobleman's son."

ERMIN: *see* Herman.

ERNEST: (Teutonic) "sincere; intent." Dim., Ern, Ernie.

ERROL: *see* Earl.

ERSKINE: (Celtic) of uncertain meaning.

ERWIN: *see* Irvin.

ESMOND: (Anglo-Saxon) "gracious protector."

ESTES: (Latin) "from a famous ruling house."

ETHAN: (Hebrew) "steadfast."

ETHELBERT: *see* Albert.

EUGENE: (Greek) "noble; well born." Dim., Gene.

EUSTACE: (Greek) "fruitful."

EVAN: *see* John.

EVELYN: (Old English) "a dear youth."

EVERARD: (Teutonic) "mighty as a boar." Var. and dim., Eberhart, Everett; Ev.

EVERETT: *see* Everard.

EWALD: (Latin) "the bearer of good news."

EWERT: (Old English) "ewe herder."

EWING: (Old English) "law friend."

EZEKIEL: (Hebrew) "God's strength." Dim., Zeke.

EZRA: (Hebrew) "the helper" or "helper." Dim., Ez.

F

FABIAN: (Latin) "prosperous farmer." Dim., Fabe.

FABRON: (South French) "little blacksmith."

FAGAN: (Irish Gaelic) "little fiery one."

FAIRFAX: (Anglo-Saxon) "fair" or "yellow-haired."

FAIRLEY: (Anglo-Saxon) "from the far meadow." Var. and dim., Fairlie, Farley; Farl.

FALKNER: (Anglo-Saxon) "falcon hunter" or "trainer." Var., Faulkner, Fowler.

FANE: (Old English) "glad; joyful."

FARAND: (Teutonic) "attractive; pleasant." Var. and dim., Farant, Farrand; Ran.

FARLEY: *see* Fairley.

FARNELL: (Old English) "from the fern slope." Var., Fernald.

FARNHAM: (Old English) "from the fern field."

FARNLEY: (Old English) "from the fern meadow."

FAROLD: (Old English) "mighty traveler."

FARR: (Old English) "traveler."

FARRAND: *see* Farand.

FARRELL: (Celtic) "the valorous one." Var., Farrel.

FAULKNER: *see* Falkner.

FAUST: (Latin) "lucky, auspicious."

FAVIAN: (Latin) "a man of understanding."

FAXON: (Teutonic) "renowned for his hair."

FAY: (Irish Gaelic) "raven."

FELIX: (Latin) "fortunate."

FELTON: (Old English) "from the field estate."

FENTON: (Anglo-Saxon) "dweller of the marshland."

FEODOR: *see* Theodore.

FERDINAND: (Teutonic) "bold venture." Var. and dim., Fernand, Fernando, Hernando; Ferd, Ferde, Ferdie.

FERGUS: (Celtic) "best choice" or "strong man."

FERNALD: *see* Farnell.

FERNAND, FERNANDO: *see* Ferdinand.

FERRIS: (Celtic) "rock."

FIDEL: (Latin) "faithful."

FIELDING: (Old English) "dweller at the field."

FILBERT: (Old English) "very brilliant one." *See also* Philbert.

FILMER: (Old English) "very famous one." Var., Filmore.

FILMORE: *see* Filmer.

FINDLAY: *see* Finley.

FINLEY: (Irish Gaelic) "little fair-haired valorous one." Var., Findlay.

FINN: (Irish Gaelic) "fair-haired and -complexioned."

FIRMAN: (Anglo-Saxon) "traveler to distant places."

FISK: (Scandinavian) "the fisherman." Var., Fiske.

FITCH: (Middle English) "European ermine or marten."

FITZGERALD: (Teutonic) "a son of Gerald."

FITZHUGH: (Old English) "son of the intelligent one."

FITZPATRICK: (Teutonic) "a son of Patrick."

FLAVIAN: (Latin) "fair" or "blond." Var., Flavius.

FLAVIUS: (Latin) "golden yellow hair."

FLEMING: (Anglo-Saxon) "the Dutchman." Dim., Flem.

FLETCHER: (French) "arrow maker." Dim., Fletch.

FLORIAN: (Latin) "flowering; blooming." Dim., Flory.

FLOYD: *see* Lloyd.

FORBES: (Irish Gaelic) "man of prosperity."

FORD: *see* Bradford.

FORREST: (Teutonic) "from the woods." Var., Forest.

FORRESTER: (Middle English) "forest guardian."

FORTUNE: (Old French) "lucky one."

FOSTER: (Teutonic) "forester; keeper of the preserve."

FOWLER: *see* Falkner.

FRANCIS: (Teutonic) "free." Var. and dim., Franchot, Franz; Frank, Frankie, Fran.

FRANK: *see* Francis, Franklin.

FRANKLIN: (Teutonic) "a free man." Dim., Frank.

FRANZ: *see* Francis.

FRASER: *see* Frazer.

FRAZER: (Old French) "strawberry." Var., Frazer.

FRAYNE: (Middle English) "stranger."

FREDERICK: (Teutonic) "peaceful chieftain." Var. and dim., Frederic, Fredric; Fred, Freddie, Freddy, Fritz.

FREEMAN: (Anglo-Saxon) "one born free." Var., Freemon.

FREMONT: (Old German) "free or noble protector."

FREWIN: (Old English) "free, noble friend."

FREY: (Old English) "lord."

FRICK: (Old English) "bold man."

FRIDOLF: (Old English) "peaceful wolf."

FRITZ: *see* Frederick.

FULLER: (Middle English) "cloth-thickener."

FULTON: (Anglo-Saxon) "from a field" or "farm town."

FYFE: (Pictish-Scotch) "from Fifeshire, Scotland."

G

GABLE: (Old French) "little Gabriel."

GABRIEL: (Hebrew) "God is mighty." Dim., Gabby, Gabe.

GADMAN: (Hebrew) "the fortunate." Var., Gadmon.

GAGE: (Old French) "pledge."

GAIR: (Irish Gaelic) "short one."

GALE: (Celtic) "lively."

GALEN: (Greek) "healer."

GALLAGHER: (Irish Gaelic) "eager helper."

GALLOWAY: (Old Gaelic) "man from the land of Gaels."

GALTON: (Old English) "owner of a rented estate."

GALVIN: (Celtic) "the sparrow." Dim., Vin, Vinny.

GAMALIEL: (Hebrew) "the Lord is my recompense."

GANNON: (Irish Gaelic) "little fair-complexioned one."

GAR: dim. of any name beginning with "Gar"; also used as an independent name.

GARDINER: (Teutonic) "flower-lover." Var., Gardner.

GARETT: (Anglo-Saxon) "mighty spear." Var. and dim., Gareth, Garreth, Garrett, Garth, Gerard, Jaret; Garey, Garry, Gary, Gerry, Jary.

GAREY: *see* Garett.

GARFIELD: (Old English) "triangular field."

GARIBALD: (Old English) "a welcome addition."

GARLAND: (Old English) "from the spear land."

GARMAN: (Old English) "spearman."

GARMOND: (Old English) "spear protector."

GARNER: (Teutonic) "the defender; noble guardian."

GARNET: (Latin) "grain; red jewel." Var., Garnett.

GARNOCK: (Old Welsh) "dweller by the alder river."

GARRICK: (Teutonic) "mighty warrior." Dim., Rick.

GARROWAY: (Old English) "spear warrior."

GARTH: (Anglo-Saxon) "yard-keeper." *See also* Garett.

GARTON: (Old English) "dweller at the triangular farmstead."

GARVEY: (Irish Gaelic) "rough peace."

GARVIN: (Teutonic) "battle friend." Dim., Gar, Gary.

GARWOOD: (Old English) "from the fir forest."

GARY: *see* Garett, Garvin.

GASPAR: *see* Jasper.

GASTON: (Teutonic) "from Gascony."

GAVIN: *see* Gawain.

GAWAIN: (Teutonic) "battle hawk." Var., Gavin.

GAYLORD: (Anglo-Saxon) "the joyous nobleman."

GAYNOR: (Irish Gaelic) "son of the fair-head."

GEARY: (Middle English) "changeable one."

GEBER: (Hebrew) "strong."

GENE: *see* Eugene.

GEOFFREY: (Teutonic) "God's peace; peace of the land."
Var. and dim., Godfrey, Jeffers, Jeffery, Jeffrey, Jeffry;
Geof, Geoff, Jeff.

GEORGE: (Greek) "farmer; tiller of the soil." Var. and
dim., Gustaf, Gustavus, Jorge, Jurgen; Gus, Gussie. *See
also* August.

GERALD: (Teutonic) "mighty spearman." Var. and dim.,
Garold, Gereld, Gerrald, Jereld, Jerold, Jerrold; Gerry,
Gery, Jer, Jerry.

GERARD: *see* Garett.

GERRY: *see* Garett, Gerald, Jermyn.

GERVASE: (Teutonic) "spear vassal" or "honorable."
Var. and dim., Gervais, Jarvis, Jervis; Jarv, Jarvey.

GIAN: *see* John.

GIBSON: (Old English) "son of Gilbert."

GIDEON: (Hebrew) "brave warrior; indomitable spirit."

GIFFORD: (Teutonic) "gift."

GILBERT: (Teutonic) "bright pledge." Var. and dim.,
Gilpin, Wilbert, Wilbur; Gil.

GILBY: (Old Norse) "hostage's estate."

GILCHRIST: (Irish Gaelic) "servant of Christ."

GILES: (Latin) "shield bearer." Var. and dim., Gile,
Gilles; Gil, Gilly.

GILMER: (Old English) "famous hostage."

GILMORE: (Irish Gaelic) "adherent of St. Mary."

GILROY: (Latin) "the king's faithful servant."

GIOVANNI: *see* John.

GIRVIN: (Irish Gaelic) "little rough one."

GLADWIN: *see* Goodwin.

GLANVILLE: (Old French) "from the oak-tree estate."

GLEN: (Celtic) "from the valley." Var., Glenn, Glynn.

GODDARD: (Teutonic) "of a firm nature." Var., Godderd,
Goddord.

GODFREY: *see* Geoffrey.

GOLDING: (Old English) "son of the golden one."

GOLDWIN: (Old English) "golden friend."

GOODMAN: (Teutonic) "good man."

GOODWIN: (Teutonic) "good and faithful friend." Var., Gladwin, Godwin.

GORDON: (Anglo-Saxon) "from the cornered hill."

GORMAN: (Irish-Gaelic) "little blue-eyed one."

GOUVERNEUR: (French) "governor."

GOWER: (Old Welsh) "pure one."

GRADY: (Irish Gaelic) "noble, illustrious."

GRAHAM: (Teutonic) "from the gray home." Var. and dim., Graeme; Ham.

GRANGER: (Old English) "farmer."

GRANT: (French) "great."

GRANTLAND: (Old English) "from the great grassy plain."

GRANVILLE: (French) "of the big town."

GRAYSON: (Old English) "a judge's son." Var. and dim., Greyson; Gray, Grey.

GREELEY: (Old English) "from the gray meadow."

GREGORY: (Greek) "vigilant." Dim., Greg.

GRESHAM: (Anglo-Saxon) "from the grazing land."

GRIFFITH: (Celtic) "red-haired." Var. and dim., Griffin, Rufus; Griff, Rufe.

GRISWOLD: (Teutonic) "from the wild gray forest."

GROVER: (Anglo-Saxon) "grove-dweller."

GUNTHER: (Teutonic) "bold warrior." Var., Gunar, Guntar, Gunter, Gunthar.

GUS: *see* Angus, Argus, August, George, Gustave.

GUSTAVE: (Scandinavian) "noble staff." Var. and dim., Gustaf, Gustavus; Gus, Gussie. *See also* August, George.

GUSTIN: *see* August.

GUTHRIE: (Celtic) "war serpent" or "war hero."

GUY: (French) "guide." Var., Guido, Guyon, Wiatt, Wyatt.

GWYN: (Celtic) "fair."

H

HACKETT: (Old Franco-German) "little hacker."

HADDEN: (Old English) "of the moors." Var., Haden.

HADLEY: (Old English) "from the heath meadow."

HADRIAN: *see* Adrian.

HADWIN: (Old English) "war-friend."

HAGEN: (Irish Gaelic) "little; young one."

HAGLEY: (Old English) "from the hedged pasture."

HAIG: (Old English) "dweller at the hedged enclosure."

HAINES: (Teutonic) "from a vined cottage." Var., Haynes.

HAKON: (Old Norse) "of the high race."

HAL: *see* Harold, Henry.

HALBERT: (Old English) "brilliant hero."

HALDEN: (Teutonic) "half Dane." Var., Haldane.

HALE: (Old English) "from a sturdy stock."

HALEY: (Irish Gaelic) "ingenious."

HALFORD: (Old English) "from the hill-slope ford."

HALL: (Old English) "from the master's house."

HALLEY: (Old English) "from the manor house meadow."

HALLIWELL: (Old English) "dweller by a holy spring."

HALLWARD: (Old English) "hall warden."

HALDSEY: (Anglo-Saxon) "from Hal's island." Var., Halsy.

HALSTEAD: (Old English) "from the manor house place."

HALTON: (Old English) "from the hill-slope estate."

HAMAL: (Arabic) "lamb."

HAMAR: (Old Norse) "a symbol of the ingenuity of man."

HAMILTON: (French) "from the mountain hamlet."

HAMISH: *see* James.

HAMLET: (Old Franco-German) "little home."

HAMLIN: *see* Henry.

HANFORD: (Old English) "from the high ford."

HANK: *see* Henry.

HANLEY: (Anglo-Saxon) "of the high meadow." Var., Hanleigh, Henleigh, Henley, Henry.

HANS: *see* John.

HANSEL: (Scandinavian) "a gift from the Lord."

HARBERT: *see* Herbert.

HARBIN: (Old Franco-German) "small, glorious warrior."

HARCOURT: (French) "from an armed court."

HARDEN: (Old English) "from the hare valley."

HARDING: (Old English) "brave one's son."

HARDWIN: (Old English) "brave friend."

HARDY: (Teutonic) "of hardy stock."

HARFORD: (Old English) "from the hare ford."

HARGROVE: (Old English) "from the hare grove."

HARIM: (Hebrew) "flat-nosed."

HARLAN: (Teutonic) "from the battle land."

HARLEY: (Anglo-Saxon) "from the hare's" or "stag's meadow." Var. and dim., Harden, Harleigh, Hartley; Arley, Arlie, Harl, Hart.

HARLOW: (Old English) "fortified hill."

HARMAN, HARMON: *see* Herman.

HAROD: (Hebrew) "the loud terror." Var., Harrod.

HAROLD: (Anglo-Saxon) "army commander." Var. and dim., Harald, Herald, Hereld, Herold, Herrick; Hal, Harry.

HARPER: (Old English) "harp player."

HARRIS: (Old English) "a son of Henry."

HARRY: *see* Harold, Henry.

HART: (Old English) "hart deer." *See also* Harley, Hartwell.

HARTFORD: (Old English) "stag ford."

HARTLEY: *see* Harley.

HARTMAN: (Old German) "strong man."

HARTWELL: (Teutonic) "from the deer's spring." Var. and dim., Harwell, Harwill; Hart.

HARTWOOD: (Old English) "hart deer forest."

HARVEY: (French) "bitter." Var. and dim., Hervey; Harv, Harve, Herv, Herve.

HASLETT: (Old English) "hazel-tree headland."

HASTINGS: (Old English) "son of the violent one."

HAVELOCK: (Old Norse) "sea contest."

HAVEN: (Old English) "place of safety."

HAWLEY: (Old English) "from the hedged meadow."

HAYDEN: (Teutonic) "from the hedged hill."

HAYES: (Old English) "from the woods; the hunter."

HAYWARD: (Old English) "hedged enclosure keeper."

HAYWOOD: (Old English) "from the hedged forest."

HEATH: (Anglo-Saxon) "from the vast wasteland."

HEATHCLIFF: (Middle English) "from the heath cliff."

HECTOR: (Greek) "steady; unswerving." Dim., Heck.

HEINRICK, HENDRICK, HENDRIK: *see* Henry.

HENLEY: *see* Hanley.

HENRY: (Teutonic) "home ruler." Var. and dim., Enrico, Hamlin, Heinrick, Hendrick, Hendrik, Henri; Hal, Hank, Harry, Hen. *See also* Hanley.

HERALD: *see* Harold.

HERBERT: (Teutonic) "bright warrior." Var. and dim., Harbert; Bert, Bertie, Herb, Herbie.

HERMAN: (Teutonic) "noble warrior." Var. and dim., Armand, Armin, Armond, Armyn, Ermin, Harman, Harmon, Hermon; Herm, Hermie.

HERNANDO: *see* Ferdinand.

HERRICK: (Old German) "army ruler." *See also* Harold.

HERROD: (Hebrew) "heroic conqueror." Var., Herod.

HERVEY: *see* Harvey.

HERWIN: (Teutonic) "a friend" or "lover of battle."

HEWE: *see* Hugh.

HEWETT: (Old Franco-German) "little Hugh."

HEYWOOD: (Teutonic) "from the dark, green forest."

HEZEKIAH: (Hebrew) "God is strength." Var., Hesketh.

HIATT: *see* Hyatt.

HILARY: (Latin) "cheerful; merry." Var., Hilaire, Hillary.

HILDEBRAND: (Old German) "war sword."

HILLEL: (Hebrew) "greatly praised."

HILLIARD: (Teutonic) "war guardian" or "protector."

HILTON: (Old English) "from the house on the hill."

HIRAM: (Hebrew) "most noble; exalted." Dim., Hy.

HOBART: *see* Hubert.

HOGAN: (Irish Gaelic) "youth."

HOLBROOK: (Anglo-Saxon) "from the valley brook."

HOLCOMB: (Old English) "deep valley."

HOLDEN: (Teutonic) "kind."

HOLLIS: (Anglo-Saxon) "dweller by the holly trees."

HOLMES: (Middle English) "from the river islands."

HOLT: (Old English) "from the forest."

HOMER: (Greek) "pledge."

HORACE: (Latin) "timekeeper." Var. and dim., Horatio, Horatius; Race.

HORATIO: *see* Horace.

HORTON: (Old English) "from the gray estate."

HOSEA: (Hebrew) "salvation."

HOUGHTON: (Old English) "from the estate on the bluff."

HOUSTON: (Anglo-Saxon) "from a mountain town."

HOWARD: (Teutonic) "chief guardian." Dim., Howie.

HOWE: (Old German) "eminent one."

HOWELL: (Old Welsh) "little alert one."

HOWLAND: (Old English) "of the hills."

HOYT: *see* Hubert.

HUBERT: (Teutonic) "shining of mind." Var. and dim., Hobart, Hoyt, Hubbard; Hubie.

HUGH: (Teutonic) "mind; intelligence." Var. and dim., Hewe, Hughes, Hugo; Huey, Hughie.

HUGO: *see* Hugh.

HUMBERT: (Teutonic) "bright home." Dim., Bert, Bertie.

HUME: (Teutonic) "lover of his home."

HUMPHREY: (Teutonic) "a protector of the peace." Var., Humfrey.

HUNTER: (Old English) "the hunter." Var., Huntley.

HUNTINGDON: (Old English) "hunter's hill."

HUNTINGTON: (Old English) "hunting estate."

HUNTLEY: (Old English) "from the hunter's meadow." *See also* Hunter.

HURLBERT: (Old English) "brilliant army leader."

HURLEY: (Irish Gaelic) "sea tide."

HURST: (Middle English) "dweller at the forest."

HUTTON: (Old English) "from the estate on the projecting ridge."

HUXFORD: (Old English) "Hugh's ford."

HUXLEY: (Old English) "Hugh's meadow."

HYATT: (Old English) "from the high gate." Var., Hiatt.

HYDE: (Old English) "from the acreage that supported one family."

HYMAN: (Hebrew) "life." Masculine of Eve. Var. and dim., Hymen; Hy, Hymie.

IAN: *see* John.

ICHABOD: (Hebrew) "the glory has departed."

IGNATIUS: (Latin) "the fiery and ardent." Var. and dim., Ignace, Ignatz; Iggy.

IGOR: (Scandinavian) "hero." Var., Inge, Ingmar.

IMMANUEL: *see* Emmanuel.

INGEMAR: (Old Norse) "famous son."

INGLEBERT: (Old German) "angel brilliant."

INGRAM: (Teutonic) "the raven." Var., Ingraham.

INNESS: (Celtic) "from the island." Var., Innis.

IRA: (Hebrew) "watcher."

IRVIN: (Anglo-Saxon) "sea friend." Var. and dim., Ervin, Ervine, Erwin, Irving, Irwin, Marvin, Mervin, Merwin; Irv, Marv, Merv.

IRVING: *see* Irvin.

IRWIN: *see* Irvin.

ISAAC: (Hebrew) "laughing."

ISHAM: (Old English) "from the iron one's estate."

ISIDORE: (Greek) "a gift." Var. and dim., Isador, Isadore, Isidor; Dore, Dorian, Dory, Issy, Iz, Izzy.

ISMAN: (Hebrew) "a loyal husband."

ISRAEL: (Hebrew) "the Lord's warrior" or "soldier." Dim., Issy, Iz, Izzy.

IVAN: *see* John.

IVAR: (Scandinavian) "military archer." Var., Iver, Ives, Ivo, Ivon, Ivor, Yves.

IVEN: (Old French) "little yew-bow."

IVES: *see* Ivar, Yves.

J

JABEZ: (Hebrew) "cause of sorrow." Dim., Jabe.

JACK: *see* James, John.

JACKSON: (Old English) "son of Jack."

JACOB: *see* James.

JACQUES: *see* James.

JAGGER: (North English) "carter; teamster."

JAMES: (Hebrew) "the supplanter." Var. and dim., Diego,

Hamish, Jacob, Jacques, Seamus, Shamus; Jack, Jake, Jakie, Jamesy, Jamie, Jem, Jemmie, Jemmy, Jim, Jimmie, Jimmy, Jock, Jocko.

JAN: *see* John.

JARED: (Hebrew) "the descending" or "descendant."

JARLATH: (Latin) "man of control."

JARMAN: (Old German) "the German."

JARVIS: *see* Gervase.

JASON: (Greek) "healer."

JASPER: (Persian) "treasure bringer." Var. and dim., Casper, Gaspar, Kaspar; Cass.

JAVIER: *see* Xavier.

JAY: (Anglo-Saxon) "crow" or "lively." Also used as a dim. for names beginning with the initial *J*.

JEAN: *see* John.

JECONIAH: (Hebrew) "gift of the Lord."

JED: (Hebrew) "beloved of the lord."

JEDEDIAH: (Hebrew) "beloved by the Lord." Var. and dim., Jedidiah; Jed, Jeddy.

JEFFERSON: (Old English) "son of Jeffrey."

JEFFREY: *see* Geoffrey.

JEGAR: (Hebrew) "witness our love." Var., Jeggar, Jegger.

JERELD, JEROLD, JERROLD: *see* Gerald.

JEREMIAH: *see* Jeremy.

JEREMY: (Hebrew) "exalted by the Lord." Var. and dim., Jeremiah, Jeremias; Jerry.

JERMYN: (Latin) "a German." Var. and dim., Germaine, Jermaine; Gerry, Jer, Jerry.

JEROME: (Greek) "holy." Dim., Jer, Jerry.

JERVIS: *see* Gervase.

JESSE: (Hebrew) "God's gift" or "grace." Dim., Jess.

JETHRO: (Hebrew) "outstanding; excellent." Dim., Jeth.

JEVON: *see* John.

JIM: *see* James.

JOAB: (Hebrew) "praise the Lord."

JOACHIM: (Hebrew) "the Lord will judge."

JOB: (Hebrew) "the persecuted; the afflicted."

JOCK: *see* James, John.

JOEL: (Hebrew) "Jehovah is God." Dim., Joe, Joey.

JOHAN, JOHANN: *see* John.

JOHN: (Hebrew) "God's gracious gift." Var. and dim., Evan, Gian, Giovanni, Hans, Ian, Ivan, Jan, Jean, Jevon, Johan, Johann, Jon, Juan, Sean, Shane, Shawn, Zane; Jack, Jock, Johnnie, Johnny, Jonnie, Jonny.

JONAH: (Hebrew) "peace." *See also* Jonas.

JONAS: (Hebrew) "dove." Var., Jonah, Jone.

JONATHAN: (Hebrew) "gift of the Lord." Dim., Jon.

JORDAN: (Hebrew) "descending."

JORGE: *see* George.

JOSEPH: (Hebrew) "He shall add." Var. and dim., Jose; Joe, Joey, Jos.

JOSES: (Hebrew) "helped by the Lord."

JOSHUA: (Hebrew) "whom God has saved." Dim., Josh.

JOSIAH: (Hebrew) "he is healed by the Lord."

JOTHAM: (Hebrew) "God is perfect." Dim., Joe.

JUAN: *see* John.

JUDD: (Hebrew) "descendant."

JUDSON: (Teutonic) "the son of Judd."

JULES: *see* Julius.

JULIAN: *see* Julius.

JULIUS: (Latin) "divinely youthful." Var. and dim., Joliet, Jules, Julian; Jule, Juley, Julie.

JUNIUS: (Latin) "born in June." Dim., June, Junie.

JURGEN: *see* George.

JUSTIN: (Latin) "the just." Var. and dim., Justus, Just.

JUSTIS: (Old French) "justice."

K

KANE: (Celtic) "bright; radiant." Var., Kayne.

KARL: *see* Charles.

KASPAR: *see* Jasper.

KAVAN: *see* Cavan.

KAY: (Latin) "rejoiced in." Also used as a dim. for names beginning with *K*.

KEANE: (Middle English) "bold, sharp one."

KEDAR: (Arabic) "powerful."

KEEFE: (Irish Gaelic) "handsome, noble, gentle, lovable."

KEEGAN: (Irish Gaelic) "little fiery one."

KEELAN: (Irish Gaelic) "little slender one."

KEELEY: (Irish Gaelic) "handsome."

KEENAN: (Irish Gaelic) "little ancient one."

KEITH: (Celtic) "a place."

KELL: (Old Norse) "from the spring."

KELLER: (Irish Gaelic) "little companion."

KELLY: (Irish Gaelic) "warrior."

KELSEY: (Teutonic) "from the water." Var., Kelcey.

KELVIN: (Irish Gaelic) "from the narrow river."

KEMP: (Middle English) "champion."

KENDALL: (Celtic) "chief of the valley." Var. and dim., Kendal; Ken, Kenny.

KENDRICK: (Anglo-Saxon) "royal ruler." Var. and dim., Kendricks, Kenric; Ken.

KENELM: (Anglo-Saxon) "brave helmet." Dim., Ken.

KENLEY: (Old English) "of the king's meadow." Var., Kenleigh.

KENNARD: (Old English) "bold, strong."

KENNETH: (Celtic) "handsome." Var. and dim., Kennet, Ken, Kenny, Kent.

KENRICK: (Old English) "bold ruler."

KENT: *see* Kenneth.

KENTON: (Old English) "from the royal estate."

KENWARD: (Old English) "bold guardian."

KENWAY: (Anglo-Saxon) "the brave soldier." Dim., Ken, Kenny.

KENYON: (Celtic) "fair-haired." Dim., Ken, Kenny.

KERBY: *see* Kirby.

KERMIT: (Celtic) "free." Var. and dim., Dermot; Kerry.

KERN: (Irish Gaelic) "little dark one."

KERR: (Celtic) "dark; mysterious." Var. and dim., Kerrin, Kieran; Kerrie, Kerry. *See also* Kirby.

KERWIN: (Irish Gaelic) "little jet-black one." Var., Kirwin.

KESTER: *see* Christopher.

KEVIN: (Celtic) "kind; gentle." Dim., Kev.

KEY: (Irish Gaelic) "son of the fiery one."

KIERAN: (Irish Gaelic) "little dark-complexioned one." *See also* Kerr.

KILLIAN: (Irish Gaelic) "little warlike one."

KIM: *see* Kimball.

KIMBALL: (Anglo-Saxon) "royally brave." Var. and dim., Kemble, Kimble; Kim.

KING: (Anglo-Saxon) "king."

KINGSLEY: (Anglo-Saxon) "from the king's meadow."

KINGSTON: (Old English) "dweller at the king's estate."

KINGSWELL: (Old English) "dweller at the king's spring."

KINNARD: (Irish Gaelic) "from the high hill."

KINNELL: (Irish Gaelic) "from the head of the cliff."

KINSEY: (Old English) "victorious one."

KIPP: (North English) "dweller at the pointed hill."

KIRBY: (Teutonic) "from the church village." Var. and dim., Kerby; Kerr.

KIRK: (Scandinavian) "of the church; living close to the church." Var., Kerk.

KIRKLEY: (Old North English) "church meadow."

KIRKWOOD: (Old North English) "from the church forest."

KIRWIN: *see* Kerwin.

KIT: *see* Christian, Christopher.

KLAUS: *see* Nicholas.

KNIGHT: (Middle English) "soldier."

KNOX: (Old English) "from the hills."

KNUTE: (Danish) "kind."

KONRAD: *see* Conrad.

KURT: *see* Curtis.

KYLE: (Gaelic) "fair and handsome." Var., Kile.

KYNAN: *see* Conal.

KYNE: (Old English) "royal one."

L

LABAN: (Hebrew) "white."

LACH: (Old English) "dweller by the water."

LACHLAN: (Celtic) "warlike."

LACY: (Latin) "from Latius; estate."

LADD: (Middle English) "attendant."

LAIBROOK: (Old English) "path by the brook."

LAIDLEY: (Old English) "from the watercourse meadow."

LAIRD: (Celtic) "proprietor."

LAMAR: (Old German) "land famous."

LAMBERT: (Teutonic) "rich in land." Dim., Bert, Lam.

LAMONT: (Scandinavian) "a lawyer." Var., Lamond.

LANCE: (Anglo-Saxon) "spear." Var. and dim., Lancelot, Launce, Launcelot; Lancey.

LANDER: (Middle English) "owner of a grassy plain."

LANDON: (Anglo-Saxon) "from the long hill." Var.; Langdon, Langston.

LANE: (Anglo-Saxon) "from the country road."

LANG: (Teutonic) "tall."

LANGDON: *see* Landon.

LANGFORD: (Old English) "dweller at the long ford."

LANGLEY: (Old English) "from the long meadow."

LANGSTON: (Old English) "tall man's town." *See also* Landon.

LANGWORTH: (Old English) "from the long enclosure."

LARRY: *see* Lawrence.

LARS, LARZ: *see* Lawrence.

LARSON: (Scandinavian) "son of Lars."

LATHAM: (Old Norse) "from the barns."

LATHROP: (Anglo-Saxon) "of the village." Var., Lathrope.

LATIMER: (Anglo-Saxon) "Latin master or teacher."

LAUNCELOT: *see* Lance.

LAUREN, LAURENCE, LAURENT: *see* Lawrence.

LAWFORD: (Old English) "from the ford at the hill."

LAWLER: (Irish Gaelic) "mumbler."

LAWLEY: (Old English) "from the hill meadow."

LAWRENCE: (Latin) "laurel; crowned with laurel." Var. and dim., Lauren, Laurence, Laurent, Loren, Lorenz, Lorenzo, Lorin; Larry, Lars, Larz, Laurie, Lori, Lorry.

LAWSON: (Old English) "son of Lawrence."

LAWTON: (Old English) "man of refinement." Var., Laughton.

LAZARUS: *see* Eleazer.

LEAL: (Middle English) "loyal."

LEANDER: (Greek) "lion-man; brave." Dim., Lee.

LEAR: (Teutonic) "of the meadow."

LEE: (Anglo-Saxon) "meadow; sheltered." Var., Leigh. Also used as dim. of Ashley, Leander, Leo, Leopold, etc.

LEGGETT: (Old French) "envoy or delegate."

LEICESTER: *see* Lester.

LEIF: (Old Norse) "beloved one."

LEIGH: *see* Lee.

LEIGHTON: (Old English) "dweller at the meadow farm."

LEITH: (Scotch Gaelic) "wide river."

LELAND: (Anglo-Saxon) "of the lowlands." Var., Leeland.

LEMUEL: (Hebrew) "consecrated to God." Dim., Lem.

LENNON: (Irish Gaelic) "little cloak."

LENNOX: (Scotch Gaelic) "abounding in elm trees."

LEO: (Latin) "lion; brave as a lion." Var. and dim., Leon, Leonard, Leonardo, Lion, Lionel, Lyon; Len, Lennie, Lenny. *See also* Leopold.

LEON, LEONARD, LEONARDO: *see* Leo.

LEOPOLD: (Teutonic) "brave for the people; patriotic." Dim., Lee, Leo, Lepp.

LEROY: *see* Elroy.

LES: *see* Leslie, Lester.

LESLIE: (Celtic) "from the gray fort." Var. and dim., Lesley (usually fem.), Les.

LESTER: (Anglo-Saxon) "from the army" or "camp." Var. and dim., Leicester; Les.

LEVERETT: (Old French) "young rabbit."

LEVERTON: (Old English) "from the rush farm."

LEVI: (Hebrew) "united."

LEWIS: (Teutonic) "renowned in battle." Var. and dim., Aloysius, Clovis, Lewes, Louis, Ludovick, Ludvig, Luigi, Luis; Lew, Lou, Louie.

LINCOLN: (Celtic) "from the place by the pool; riverbank." Dim., Linc, Link.

LIND: (Old English) "dweller at the lime tree."

LINDBERG: (Old German) "linden-tree hill."

LINDELL: (Old English) "dweller at the linden-tree valley."

LINDLEY: (Old English) "at the linden-tree meadow."

111

LINDON: *see* Lyndon.

LINDSEY: (Old English) "pool island."

LINFORD: (Old English) "from the linden-tree ford."

LINK: (Old English) "from the bank." *See also* Lincoln.

LINLEY: (Old English) "from the flax enclosure."

LINUS: (Hebrew) "flaxen-haired."

LIONEL: *see* Leo.

LITTON: (Old English) "hillside town."

LLEWELLYN: (Celtic) "lionlike; lightning."

LLOYD: (Celtic) "gray" or "dark." Var., Floyd.

LOCKE: (Old English) "dweller by the stronghold."

LOGAN: (Scotch Gaelic) "little hollow."

LOMBARK: (Latin) "long-bearded one."

LON, LONNY: *see* Alphonse, Zebulon.

LOREN, LORENZO, LORRY: *see* Lawrence, Loring.

LORIMER: (Latin) "lover of horses."

LORING: (Teutonic) "coming from Lorraine." Var. and dim., Loredo, Loren, Lorry.

LOT: (Hebrew) "veiled."

LOTHAR: *see* Luther.

LOUIS: *see* Lewis.

LOWELL: (Anglo-Saxon) "beloved." Var., Lovel, Lovell.

LOYAL: (Old French) "true, unswerving."

LUCAS: *see* Lucius.

LUCIUS: (Latin) "light." Var. and dim., Lucas, Lucian; Luce, Luke, Lukev.

LUDLOW: (Old English) "dweller at the prince's hill."

LUDOVICK, LUDVIG: *see* Lewis.

LUIGI: *see* Lewis.

LUKE: *see* Lucius.

LUNDY: (French) "born on Monday."

LUNN: (Irish Gaelic) "strong, fierce."

LUNT: (Old Norse) "from the grove."

LUTHER: (Teutonic) "renowned warrior." Var., Lothair, Lothar, Lothario.

LYLE: (French) "from the island." Var., Lisle.

LYMAN: (Old English) "man of the plains."

LYNDON: (Old English) "of the linden tree." Var., Lindon.

LYNN: (Anglo-Saxon) "from the waterfalls." Var., Linn.

LYON: *see* Leo.

LYSANDER: (Greek) "liberator." Dim., Sandy.

M

MAC: (Celtic) "the son of." Dim. for any name beginning with "Mac" or "Mc."

MacADAM: (Scotch Gaelic) "son of Adam."

MacDONALD: (Scotch Gaelic) "son of world-mighty."

MacDOUGAL: (Scotch Gaelic) "son of the dark stranger."

MacKINLEY: (Irish Gaelic) "skillful leader."

MacMURRAY: (Irish Gaelic) "son of the mariner."

MACY: (Old French) "from Matthew's estate."

MADDOCK: (Celtic) "fire" or "beneficent." Var., Maddox, Madoc.

MADEN: *see* Matthew.

MADISON: (Teutonic) "mighty in battle."

MAGEE: (Irish Gaelic) "son of the fiery one."

MAGNUS: (Latin) "great one."

MAITLAND: (Old English) "dweller at the meadowland."

MAJOR: (Latin) "greater."

MALCOLM: (Celtic) "dove."

MALIN: (Old English) "little war-mighty one."

MALLORY: (Latin) "luckless."

MALONEY: (Irish Gaelic) "devoted to Sunday worship."

MALVIN: (Celtic) "chief." Var. and dim., Melvin; Mal.

MANDEL: (German) "almond."

MANFRED: (Old English) "peaceful man."

MANNING: (Old English) "son of the hero."

MANSFIELD: (Old English) "from the field by the small river."

MANTON: (Old English) "from the hero's estate."

MANUEL: *see* Emmanuel.

MANVILLE: (Old French) "from the great estate."

MARCEL: (Latin) "little hammer." *See also* Mark.

MARCO, MARCUS: *see* Mark.

MARDEN: (Old English) "from the pool valley."

MARIO: (Latin) "martial one."

MARION: (Old French) "little Mary."

MARK: (Latin) "belonging to Mars; a warrior." Var. and dim., Marc, Marcel, March, Marco, Marcus, Marcy, Marek, Mars, Martin, Martyn; Marty.

MARLAND: (Old English) "from the lake land."

MARLEN, MARLIN, MARLON: *see* Merlin.

MARLEY: (Old English) "from the lake meadow."

MARLOW: (Old English) "from the hill by the lake."

MARMADUKE: (Celtic) "sea leader." Dim., Duke.

MARMION: (Old French) "very small one."

MARSDEN: (Anglo-Saxon) "from the marsh valley." Dim., Denny.

MARSH: (Old English) "from the marshy spot."

MARSHALL: (French) "marshal." Var. and dim., Marshal; Marsh.

MARSTON: (Old English) "dweller at the lake farm."

MARTIN: *see* Mark.

MARVIN: *see* Irvin.

MARWOOD: (Old English) "from the lake forest."

MASLIN: (Old French) "little Thomas."

MASON: (Latin) "worker in stone."

MATHER: (Old English) "powerful army."

MATTHEW: (Hebrew) "God's gift." Var. and dim., Maddis, Maden, Mathias, Matthias; Mat, Matt, Matty.

MAURICE: (Latin) "dark; Moorish." Var. and dim.,

Morel, Morice, Morris, Murray, Seymour; Maurey, Maury, Morry.

MAXIMILLIAN: (Latin) "the greatest." Var. and dim., Maxim; Max, Maxey, Maxie.

MAXWELL: (Anglo-Saxon) "he lives near the spring."

MAYER: (Latin) "greater one."

MAYFIELD: (Old English) "from the warrior's field."

MAYHEW: (Old French) "gift of Jehovah."

MAYNARD: (Anglo-Saxon) "mightily strong."

MAYO: (Irish Gaelic) "from the plain of the yew trees."

MEAD: (Old English) "from the meadow."

MEDWIN: (Teutonic) "strong friend." Dim., Winnie.

MELBOURNE: (Old English) "from the mill stream."

MELDON: (Old English) "dweller at the mill hill."

MELVILLE: (French) "a place." Dim., Mel.

MELVIN: *see* Malvin.

MENDEL: (East Semitic) "knowledge, wisdom."

MERCER: (Latin) "merchant."

MEREDITH: (Celtic) "sea protector." Var., Meridith.

MERLE: (Latin) "blackbird." Var., Merl.

MERLIN: (Anglo-Saxon) "hawk; falcon." Var. and dim., Marlen, Marlin, Marlon; Marl, Merl.

MERRICK: *see* Emory.

MERRILL: *see* Myron.

MERRITT: (Old English) "little famous one."

MERTON: (Anglo-Saxon) "from the place by the sea."

MERVIN, MERWIN: *see* Irvin.

MEYER: (Teutonic) "farmer." Var., Mayer.

MICAH: (Hebrew) "like unto the Lord."

MICHAEL: (Hebrew) "Godlike." Var. and dim., Mitchell; Mickey, Mike, Mitch.

MILLBURN: (Old English) "of the stream by the mill."

MILES: (Greek) "millstone." Var., Milo, Myles.

MILFORD: (Old English) "dweller at the mill ford."

MILLARD: (Old English) "a miller."

MILLER: (Middle English) "grain-grinder."

MILO: (Latin) "miller." *See also* Miles.

MILTON: (Anglo-Saxon) "from the mill town." Dim., Milt.

MILWARD: (Old English) "mill keeper."

MINER: (Old French) "a miner."

MISCHA: (Hebrew) "who is like God."

MITCHELL: *see* Michael.

MODRED: (Old English) "courageous counselor."

MONROE: (Celtic) "from the red swamp." Var., Munro.

MONTAGUE: (Latin) "from the pointed mountain." Var. and dim., Montagu; Monte.

MONTE: *see* Montague, Montgomery.

MONTGOMERY: (French) "mountain hunter." Dim., Monte, Monty.

MOORE: (Old French) "dark-complexioned."

MORDECAI: (Hebrew) "a wise counselor."

MORELAND: (Old English) "from the moor land."

MORGAN: (Celtic) "from the sea" or "sea-white."

MORLEY: (Anglo-Saxon) "from the moor meadow."

MORRIS: *see* Maurice.

MORRISON: (Old English) "son of Maurice."

MORTIMER: (Latin) "from the quiet water." Dim., Mort, Mortie, Morty.

MORTON: (Anglo-Saxon) "from the moor village." Dim., Mort, Morty.

MORVEN: (Irish Gaelic) "great, blond one."

MOSES: (Egyptian) "saved from the water." Var. and dim., Mose, Moss; Moe.

MOSS: *see* Moses.

MUIR: (Celtic) "moor."

MUNRO: *see* Monroe.

MURDOCH: (Celtic) "prosperous from the sea." Var., Murdock, Murtagh.

MURPHY: (Irish Gaelic) "sea warrior."

116

MURRAY: (Celtic) "sailor." Var., Murrey, Murry. *See also* Maurice.

MYRON: (Greek) "fragrant." Var., Merrill.

N

NAIRN: (Scotch Gaelic) "dweller at the alder-tree river."

NALDO: (Teutonic) "power."

NARCISSUS: (Greek) "self-loving."

NATHANIEL: (Hebrew) "gift of God." Var. and dim., Nathan, Nathanael; Nat, Nate, Natie, Natty.

NEAL: (Celtic) "champion." Var., Neale, Neil; Nealey. *See also* Cornelius.

NED: *see* Edmund, Edward, Norton.

NELSON: (Celtic) "son of Neal." Var., Neilson. *See also* Cornelius.

NEMO: (Greek) "from the glen."

NERO: (Italian) "black; dark."

NESTOR: (Greek) "venerable wisdom." Var. and dim., Nessim; Nessie.

NEVILLE: (Latin) "from the new town." Var. and dim., Nevil; Nev.

NEVIN: (Anglo-Saxon) "nephew." Var., Nevins.

NEWEL, NEWELL: *see* Noel.

NEWLAND: (Old English) "dweller on reclaimed land."

NEWLIN: (Old Welsh) "dweller at the new pool."

NEWTON: (Anglo-Saxon) "from the new estate."

NICHOLAS: (Greek) "victory of the people." Var. and dim., Nichol, Nicholl, Nicolas, Niles; Claus, Colin, Colley, Klaus, Nick, Nicky.

NICODEMUS: (Greek) "the people's conqueror." Dim., Nick, Nicky.

NIGEL: (Latin) "dark; black."

NILES: *see* Nicholas.

NIXON: (Old English) "son of Nicholas."

NOAH: (Hebrew) "rest; comfort; peace."

NOBLE: (Latin) "renowned; noble." Var., Nobel, Nolan.

NOEL: (Latin) "Christmas." Var., Newel, Newell, Noelle.

NOLAN: *see* Noble.

NOLL: *see* Oliver.

NORBERT: (Teutonic) "sea brightness." Dim., Bert.

NORMAN: (Teutonic) "man from the north" or "of Normandy." Var. and dim., Normand, Norris; Norm, Normie.

NORRIS: *see* Norman.

NORTHCLIFF: (Old English) "from the north cliff."

NORTHROP: (Old English) "from the north farm."

NORTON: (Anglo-Saxon) "from the north place." Dim., Ned, Norty.

NORVILLE: (Old Anglo-French) "from the north estate."

NORVIN: (Teutonic) "man from the north."

NORWARD: (Teutonic) "the guard at the northern gate." Var., Norword, Norwood.

O

OAKES: (Middle English) "dweller at the oak trees."

OAKLEY: (Anglo-Saxon) "from the oak-tree meadow."

OBADIAH: (Hebrew) "the Lord's servant." Dim., Obe.

OBERT: (Old German) "wealthy, brilliant one."

OCTAVIUS: (Latin) "eighth." Var. and dim., Octave, Octavian, Octavus; Tavey.

ODELL: (Teutonic) "wealthy man." Var., Odin, Odo.

ODOLF: (Old German) "wealthy wolf."

ODORIC: (Latin) "son of a good man."

OGDEN: (Anglo-Saxon) "from the oak valley."

OGILVIE: (Pictish-Scotch) "from the high peak."

OGLESBY: (Old English) "awe-inspiring."

OLAF: (Scandinavian) "peace" or "reminder." Var., Olen.

OLIVER: (Latin) "olive; peace." Var. and dim., Olivier; Ollie, Noll, Nollie, Nolly.

OLNEY: (Old English) "Olla's island."

OMAR: (Hebrew) "talkative."

ONSLOW: (Old English) "zealous one's hill."

ORAM: (Old English) "from the riverbank enclosure."

ORDWAY: (Anglo-Saxon) "spear fighter."

OREN: (Hebrew) "pine." Var., Orin, Orrin.

ORFORD: (Old English) "dweller at the cattle ford."

ORION: (Latin) "giant."

ORLANDO: *see* Roland.

ORMOND: (Teutonic) "ship man." Var., Orman, Ormand.

ORO: (Spanish) "golden one."

ORRICK: (Old English) "dweller at the ancient oak tree."

ORSON: (Latin) "bear." Var., Orsini, Orsino.

ORTON: (Old English) "from the shore farmstead."

ORVAL: (Old English) "spear-mighty."

ORVILLE: (French) "lord of the manor." Var., Orvil.

ORVIN: (Old English) "spear friend."

OSBERT: (Anglo-Saxon) "divinely bright." Dim., Bert, Bertie, Berty, Oz, Ozzie.

OSBORN: (Anglo-Saxon) "divinely strong." Var., Osborne, Osbourne.

OSCAR: (Anglo-Saxon) "divine spear." Dim., Os, Ozzie.

OSGOOD (Teutonic) "gift of our Lord."

OSMAR: (Old English) "divinely glorious."

OSMOND: (Teutonic) "he is protected by God." Var. and dim., Osmand, Osmund; Ozzie.

OSRED: (Old English) "divine counselor."

OSRIC: (Old English) "divine ruler."

OSWALD: (Anglo-Saxon) "divine power." Dim., Os, Oz.

OTHMAN: (Old German) "prosperous man."

OTIS: (Greek) "keen-eared."

OTTO: (Teutonic) "wealthy; prosperous."
OWEN: (Celtic) "young warrior." Var., Owain.
OXFORD: (Old English) "from the oxen ford."
OXTON: (Old English) "from the ox enclosure."

P

PADDY: *see* Patrick.
PADGETT: (French) "young attendant."
PAGE: (French) "servant to the royal court." Var., Paige.
PAINE: (Latin) "countryman; rustic; pagan." Var., Payne.
PALEY: *see* Paul.
PALMER: (Latin) "the palm-bearer" or "pilgrim."
PARK: (Anglo-Saxon) "of the park." Var., Parke.
PARKER: (Middle English) "park keeper."
PARKIN: (Old English) "little Peter."
PARLE: (Old French) "little Peter."
PARNELL: *see* Peter.
PARRY: (French) "guardian; warder; protector."
PASCAL: (Italian) "born at Easter."
PATRICK: (Latin) "noble; patrician." Var. and dim.,
  Padraic, Patric, Peyton; Paddy, Pat, Patsy, Patty, Rick.
PATTON: (Old English) "from the combatant's estate."
PAUL: (Latin) "little." Var. and dim., Paley; Paulie.
PAXTON: (Teutonic) "from afar; a traveler." Var., Pack-
  ston, Paxon.
PAYNE: *see* Paine.
PAYTON: (Old English) "dweller at the fighter's estate."
PEARCE, PIERCE: *see* Peter.
PEDRO: *see* Peter.
PELL: (Old English) "mantle or scarf."
PELTON: (Old English) "from the estate by the pool."
PEMBROKE: (Celtic) "from the headland."
PENLEY: (Old English) "enclosed pasture."

120

PENN: (Old German) "commander."

PENROD: (Old German) "famous commander."

PEPIN: (Old German) "petitioner."

PERCIVAL: (French) "valley-piercer." Var. and dim., Perceval, Purcell; Perce, Percy.

PERCY: *see* Percival.

PEREGRINE: (Latin) "wanderer." Dim., Perry, Pippin.

PERRY: (Anglo-Saxon) "pear tree." Dim., Perr. *See also* Peregrine.

PERTH: (Pictish-Celtic) "thorn-bush thicket."

PETER: (Greek) "rock; stone." Var. and dim., Parnell, Pearce, Pedro, Pernell, Perrin, Petrie, Pierce, Pierre, Pietro; Pete, Petey, Petie.

PEVERELL: (Old French) "piper."

PEYTON: *see* Patrick.

PHELAN: (Celtic) "wolf; brave as a wolf."

PHILBERT: (Teutonic) "a radiant soul." Var. and dim., Filbert; Bert.

PHILIP: (Greek) "lover of horses." Var. and dim., Phelps, Phillip; Flip, Phil.

PHILO: (Greek) "love."

PHINEAS: (Hebrew) "oracle; mouth of brass."

PICKFORD: (Old English) "from the ford at the peak."

PICKWORTH: (Old English) "from the tree cutter's estate."

PIERRE: *see* Peter.

PIERSON: (Greek) "son of Peter." Var. and dim., Pearson, Peerson, Pierce.

PITNEY: (Old English) "preserving one's island."

PITTE: (Old English) "from the pit."

PIUS: (Latin) "pious."

PLATO: (Greek) "broad one."

PLATT: (Old French) "from the flat land."

POLLOCK: (Old English) "little paul."

POMEROY: (Old French) "from the apple orchard."

PORTER: (Latin) "doorkeeper" or "gatekeeper."

POWELL: (Celtic) "alert."

PRENTICE: (Latin) "learner; apprentice." Var., Prentiss.

PRESCOTT: (Anglo-Saxon) "of the priest's house."

PRESLEY: (Old English) "dweller at the priest's meadow."

PRESTON: (Anglo-Saxon) "of the priest's place."

PREWITT: (Old French) "little valiant one."

PRIMO: (Italian) "first child born to a family."

PRINCE: (Latin) "prince."

PRIOR: (Latin) "superior; head of a monastery." Var., Pryor.

PROCTOR: (Latin) "leader." Var., Procter.

PUTNAM: (Anglo-Saxon) "dweller of the pond."

Q

QUARTUS: (Latin) "fourth son."

QUENNEL: (Old French) "dweller at the little oak tree."

QUENTIN: (Latin) "fifth." Var. and dim., Quintin; Quent, Quint.

QUIGLEY: (Irish Gaelic) "distaff."

QUILLON: (Latin) "sword." Dim., Quill.

QUINBY: (Scandinavian) "of the womb of woman."

QUINCY: (Latin) "from the fifth son's place."

QUINN: *see* Conal.

QUINTON: (Latin) "fifth child."

R

RACE: *see* Horace.
RADBERT: (Old English) "brilliant counselor."
RADBURN: (Old English) "he lives by the red brook."
Var., Radbourne, Radburne.
RADCLIFFE: (Anglo-Saxon) "from the red cliff."
RADFORD: (Old English) "he lives by the red valley."
Var., Radferd, Radley.
RADNOR: (Old English) "at the red shore."
RADOLF: (Old English) "counsel wolf."
RAFAEL: *see* Raphael.
RAFFERTY: (Irish Gaelic) "prosperous and rich."
RALEIGH: (Old English) "of the deer field."
RALPH: *see* Randolph.
RALSTON: (Old English) "of the house of Ralph." Var.,
Ralfston, Roliston.
RAMBERT: (Old German) "mighty; brilliant."
RAMON: *see* Raymond.
RAMSDEN: (Old English) "raven's island."
RAMSEY: (Teutonic) "from the ram's island."
RANDALL: *see* Randolph.
RANDOLPH: (Anglo-Saxon) "protected; advised by
wolves." Var. and dim., Ralph, Randal, Randall, Rolf,
Rolfe, Rolph; Randy, Rand.
RANGER: (Old French) "forest keeper."
RANKIN: (Old English) "little shield."
RANSFORD: (Old English) "from the raven's ford."
RANSLEY: (Old English) "from the raven's meadow."
RANSON: (Old English) "son of shield."
RAOUL: (French) "swift wolf."
RAPHAEL: (Hebrew) "healed by God." Var. and dim.,
Rafael, Raffaello; Raff.

RAWLING: (Old Anglo-French) "son of the little counsel wolf." Var., Rawson.

RAWSON: (Old English) *see* Rawling.

RAYBURN: (Old English) "of the deer's brook."

RAYMOND: (Teutonic) "wise protection." Var. and dim., Ramon, Raymund; Ray. *See also* Reginald.

RAYNOR: (Old Norse) "mighty army."

READE: (Anglo-Saxon) "red-haired." Var., Reed, Reid.

READING: (Old English) "son of the red-haired one."

REDFORD: (Old English) "from the red ford."

REDLEY: (Old English) "dweller at the red meadow."

REDMOND: (Teutonic) "adviser; protector."

REDWALD: (Old English) "counsel mighty."

REECE: (Old Welsh) "ardent one."

REED: (Old English) "red-haired." *See also* Reade.

REEVE: (Middle English) "bailiff."

REGAN: (Celtic) "royal; king."

REGINALD: (Teutonic) "mighty ruler." Var. and dim., Raymond, Reinhold, Reynold, Rinaldo, Ronald; Reg, Reggie, Ron, Ronnie, Ronny.

REID: *see* Reade.

REINHOLD: *see* Reginald.

REMINGTON: (Old English) "from the raven-family estate."

REMUS: (Latin) "oarsman."

RENFRED: (Old English) "mighty and peaceful."

RENFREW: (Old Welsh) "from the still river or channel."

RENNY: (Irish Gaelic) "little; powerful."

RENSHAW: (Old English) "from the raven forest."

RENTON: (Old English) "roebuck deer estate."

REUBEN: (Hebrew) "behold a son!" Var. and dim., Ruben; Rube, Ruby.

REX: (Latin) "king."

REXFORD: (Old English) "dweller at the king's ford."

REYNARD: (Old German) "mighty; brave."

REYNOLD: (Old English) "mighty and powerful." *See also* Reginald.

RHODES: (Middle English) "dweller at the crucifixes."

RICHARD: (Teutonic) "wealthy and powerful." Var. and dim., Ricardo; Dick, Dicky, Rich, Richie, Ricky, Ritch, Ritchie.

RICHMOND: (Teutonic) "powerful protector."

RICK: a dim. of Alaric, Richard, etc., but also used as an independent name.

RICKWARD: (Old English) "powerful guardian."

RIDDOCK: (Irish Gaelic) "from the smooth field."

RIDER: (Old English) "knight or horseman." Var., Ryder.

RIDGE: (Old English) "from the ridge."

RIDGEWAY: (Old English) "from the ridge road."

RIDGLEY: (Old English) "he lives by the meadow's edge."

RIDLEY: (Old English) "from the red meadow."

RIDPATH: (Old English) "dweller on the red path."

RIGBY: (Old English) "ruler's valley."

RIGG: (Old English) "from the ridge."

RINALDO: *see* Reginald.

RING: (Old English) "a ring."

RIORDAN: (Irish Gaelic) "royal poet or bard."

RIPLEY: (Old English) "dweller at the shouter's meadow."

RISLEY: (Old English) "from the brushwood meadow."

RISTON: (Old English) "from the brushwood estate."

RITTER: (North German) "a knight."

ROALD: (Old German) "famous ruler."

ROAN: (North English) "dweller at the rowan tree."

ROARKE: (Irish Gaelic) "famous ruler."

ROBERT: (Teutonic) "of bright, shining fame." Var. and dim., Roberto, Robin, Rupert; Bob, Bobbie, Bobby, Rab, Rob, Robbie, Robby.

ROBIN: *see* Robert.

ROBINSON: (Old English) "shining with fame."

ROCHESTER: (Old English) "rocky fortress."

ROCK: (Old English) "from the rock."

ROCKLEY: (Old English) "from the rocky meadow."

ROCKWELL: (Old English) "from the rocky spring."

RODERICK: (Teutonic) "renowned ruler." Var. and dim., Broderick, Roderic, Rodrick; Rod, Roddy, Rory.

RODMANN: (Teutonic) "redhead." Var. and dim., Rodman; Rod, Roddy.

RODNEY: (Teutonic) "renowned." Dim., Rod, Roddie, Roddy, Rodi.

RODWELL: (Old English) "dweller at the crucifix spring."

ROGER: (Teutonic) "renowned spearman; famous warrior."

ROLAND: (Teutonic) "fame of the land." Var. and dim., Orlando, Rollin, Rowland; Rollo, Roley.

ROLLO: *see* Roland, Rudolph.

ROLPH: *see* Randolph, Rudolph.

ROLT: (Old German) "famous power."

ROMEO: (Latin) "pilgrim to Rome."

ROMNEY: (Old Welsh) "curving river."

ROMULUS: (Latin) "citizen of Rome."

RONALD: *see* Reginald.

RONAN: (Irish Gaelic) "little seal."

RONSON: (Old English) "son of mighty power."

ROPER: (Old English) "rope maker."

RORY: (Celtic) "ruddy; red-haired." Var., Rorie, Rorry. *See also* Roderick.

ROSCOE: (Teutonic) "from the deer forest." Dim., Ros, Roz.

ROSLIN: (Old French) "little red-haired one."

ROSS: (Teutonic) "horse."

ROSWELL: (Teutonic) "mighty steed." Dim., Ros, Roz.

ROWELL: (Old English) "from the roe deer spring."

ROWLEY: (Old English) "dweller at the rough meadow."

ROWSON: (Anglo-Irish) "son of the red-haired one."

ROXBURY: (Old English) "from rock's fortress."

ROY: (Latin) "king." *See also* Elroy.

ROYAL: (Old French) "regal one."

ROYCE: (French) "son of the king."

ROYD: (Old Norse) "from the clearing in the forest."
ROYDON: (Old English) "dweller at the rye hill."
RUBE, RUBY: *see* Reuben.
RUCK: (Old English) "rook bird."
RUDD: (Old English) "ruddy-complexioned."
RUDOLPH: (Teutonic) "famed wolf." Var. and dim., Rollin, Rudolf; Dolph, Rolfe, Rollo, Rolph, Rudy.
RUFUS: (Latin) "red-haired." Var. and dim., Griffin, Griffith; Griff, Rufe.
RUGBY: (Old English) "rook estate."
RULE: (Latin) "ruler."
RUMFORD: (Old English) "from the wide ford."
RUPERT: *see* Robert.
RUSH: (French) "red-haired."
RUSHFORD: (Old English) "from the rush ford."
RUSKIN: (Franco-German) "little redhead."
RUSS: *see* Cyrus, Russell.
RUSSELL: (Anglo-Saxon) "like a fox." Var. and dim., Russel; Russ.
RUST: (Old French) "red-haired."
RUTHERFORD: (Old English) "from the cattle ford." Var., Rutherfurd.
RUTLAND: (Old Norse) "from the root or stump land."
RUTLEDGE: (Old English) "from the red pool."
RUTLEY: (Old English) "from the stump meadow."
RYAN: (Irish Gaelic) "little king."
RYCROFT: (Old English) "from the rye field."
RYDER: *see* Rider.
RYE: (Old French) "from the riverbank."
RYLAN: (Old English) "dweller at the rye land."
RYLE: (Old English) "from the rye hill."
RYLEY: (Irish Gaelic) "valiant one."
RYMAN: (Old English) "rye seller."
RYTON: (Old English) "from the rye enclosure."

S

SABER: (French) "a sword."

SABIN: (Latin) "a man of the Sabine people."

SAFFORD: (Old English) "from the willow ford."

SALISBURY: (Old English) "from the guarded palace."

SALTON: (Old English) "from the manor-hall town."

SALVADOR: (Latin) "of the Savior." Dim., Sal.

SAMSON: (Hebrew) "sunlike." Var. and dim., Sampson, Simpson, Simson; Sam, Sammy, Sim.

SAMUEL: (Hebrew) "name of God." Dim., Sam, Sammy.

SANBORN: (Old English) "of the sandy beach." Var. and dim., Sanborne, Sanburn; Sandy.

SANCHO: (Spanish) "truthful, sincere."

SANDERS: (Greek) "son of Alexander." Var., Saunders. *See also* Alexander.

SANDY: *see* Alexander, Lysander, Sanborn, Sanford.

SANFORD: (Old English) "by the sandy crossing." Var. and dim., Sandford; Sandy.

SANTO: (Italian) "holy, sacred."

SANTON: (Old English) "sandy town."

SARGENT: (Latin) "a military attendant."

SAUL: (Hebrew) "longed for; desired."

SAVILLE: (North French) "willow estate."

SAWYER: (Celtic) "man of the woods."

SAXON: (Teutonic) "from a Saxon town." Var., Saxen.

SAYER: (Welsh) "carpenter."

SCANLON: (Irish Gaelic) "a little scandal."

SCHUYLER: (Dutch) "a scholar; a wise man."

SCOTT: (Latin) "a Scotsman." Dim., Scot, Scottie, Scotty.

SCULLY: (Irish Gaelic) "town crier."

SEABERT: (Old English) "sea-glorious."

SEABROOK: (Old English) "from the brook by the sea."

SEAMUS, SHAMUS: *see* James.

SEAN, SHAWN: *see* John.

SEARLE: (Old German) "armed one."

SEBASTIAN: (Greek) "respected; reverenced."

SEDGEWICK: (Old English) "from the village of victory." Var., Sedgewinn.

SEDGLEY: (Old English) "from the swordsman's meadow."

SEELEY: (Old English) "happy, blessed."

SEGER: (Old English) "sea warrior."

SELBY: (Teutonic) "from the manor farm." Var., Shelby.

SELDEN: (Old English) "from the willow-tree valley."

SELIG: *see* Zelig.

SELWYN: (Teutonic) "friend at the manor."

SENIOR: (Old French) "lord of the manor."

SENNETT: (French) "old, wise one."

SEPTIMUS: (Latin) "seventh son."

SERENO: (Latin) "tranquil one."

SERGE: (Latin) "the attendant."

SERLE: (Teutonic) "bearing arms" or "weapons."

SETH: (Hebrew) "chosen."

SETON: (Anglo-Saxon) "from the place by the sea."

SEVERN: (Old English) "boundary."

SEWARD: (Anglo-Saxon) "defender of the coast."

SEWELL: (Teutonic) "victorious on the sea." Var., Sewel.

SEXTON: (Middle English) "church official."

SEXTUS: (Latin) "sixth son."

SEYMOUR: (French) "follower of St. Maur." *See also* Maurice.

SHADWELL: (Old English) "from the shed spring."

SHANAHAN: (Irish Gaelic) "wise one."

SHANDY: (Old English) "little boisterous one."

SHANE: *see* John.

SHANLEY: (Irish Gaelic) "old hero."

SHANNON: (Irish Gaelic) "little old wise one."

SHATTUCK: (Middle English) "little shad fish."

SHAW: (Anglo-Saxon) "from the grove."

SHEA: (Irish Gaelic) "majestic, scientific, ingenious one."

SHEEHAN: (Irish Gaelic) "little peaceful one."

SHEFFIELD: (Old English) "from the crooked field."

SHELBY: *see* Selby.

SHELDON: (Anglo-Saxon) "from the hill ledge" or "shelly valley." Var. and dim., Shelton; Shel, Shell, Shelly.

SHELLEY: (Anglo-Saxon) "from the ledge" or "shelly meadow." Dim., Shel, Shell.

SHELTON: (Old English) "from the ledge town." *See also* Sheldon.

SHEPARD: (Anglo-Saxon) "sheep tender." Var. and dim., Shepherd, Sheppard; Shep, Shepp.

SHEPLEY: (Anglo-Saxon) "of the sheep meadow." Var. and dim., Sheply; Shep.

SHERARD: (Anglo-Saxon) "a brave soldier." Var., Sherrard.

SHERBORNE: (Old English) "from the clear brook."

SHERIDAN: (Celtic) "wild man; savage." Dim., Sherry.

SHERLOCK: (Old English) "a short-haired son."

SHERMAN: (Anglo-Saxon) "wool shearer; sheep cutter." Dim., Sherm.

SHERWIN: (Anglo-Saxon) "a true friend."

SHERWOOD: (Anglo-Saxon) "bright forest."

SHIPLEY: (Old English) "dweller at the sheep meadow."

SHIPTON: (Old English) "dweller at the sheep estate."

SHOLTO: (Irish Gaelic) "teal or merganser duck."

SIDDELL: (Old English) "from the wide valley."

SIDNEY: (French) "a follower of St. Denis." Var. and dim., Sydney; Sid, Syd.

SIGFRID: (Teutonic) "glorious peace." Var., Siegfried.

SIGMUND: (Teutonic) "victorious protector."

SIGURD: (Old Norse) "victorious guardian."

SIGWALD: (Old German) "victorious governor."

SILAS: (Latin) "of the forest." Var. and dim., Silvan, Silvanus, Silvester, Sylvan, Sylvester; Si.

SIMON: (Hebrew) "heard." Var. and dim., Simeon; Si.

SIMPSON, SIMSON: *see* Samson.

SINCLAIR: (Latin) "saintly; shining light."

SION: (Hebrew) "exalted."

SMEET: (Middle English) "swift one."

SKELLY: (Irish Gaelic) "storyteller."

SKELTON: (Old English) "from the town on the ledge."

SKERRY: (Old Norse) "from the rocky island."

SKIPP: (Old Norse) "ship owner."

SKIPTON: (Old English) "from the sheep estate."

SLADE: (Old English) "dweller in the valley."

SLEVIN: (Irish Gaelic) "mountaineer."

SLOAN: (Celtic) "warrior."

SMEDLEY: (Old English) "from the flat meadow."

SMITH: (Old English) "blacksmith."

SNOWDEN: (Old English) "from the snowy hill."

SOL: (Latin) "sun." Also used as dim. of Solomon.

SOLOMON: (Hebrew) "peaceable; wise." Dim., Sol, Solly.

SOLON: (Greek) "wise man."

SOMERSET: (Old English) "from the place of the summer settlers."

SOMERTON: (Old English) "from the summer estate."

SOMERVILLE: (Old Franco-German) "from the summer estate."

SORRELL: (Old French) "reddish-brown hair."

SOUTHWELL: (Old English) "from the south spring."

SPALDING: (Old English) "from the split meadow."

SPANGLER: (South German) "tinsmith."

SPARK: (Middle English) "gay, gallant one."

SPEAR: (Old English) "spearman."

SPEED: (Old English) "success, prosperity."

SPENCER: (French) "storekeeper; dispenser of provisions." Var. and dim., Spenser; Spence.

SPRAGUE: (Old English) "the quick one." Var., Sprage.

SQUIRE: (Middle English) "knight's attendant."

STACY: (Latin) "stable companion." Var., Stacey.

STAFFORD: (Old English) "of the landing place." Var., Staffard, Staford.

STANBURY: (Old English) "from the stone fortress."

STANCLIFF: (Old English) "from the rocky cliff."

STANDISH: (Old English) "from the rocky park."

STANFIELD: (Old English) "from the rocky field."

STANFORD: (Anglo-Saxon) "of the stony crossing."

STANHOPE: (Old English) "from the stony vale."

STANISLAUS: (Slavic) "glorious position."

STANLEY: (Slavonic) "pride of the camp." Var. and dim., Stanleigh; Lee, Stan.

STANMORE: (Old English) "from the rocky lake."

STANTON: (Anglo-Saxon) "from the stony place."

STANWAY: (Old English) "dweller on the paved stone road."

STANWICK: (Old English) "dweller at the rocky village."

STANWOOD: (Old English) "dweller at the rocky forest."

STARLING: (Old English) "sterling bird."

STARR: (Middle English) "star."

STEDMAN: (Old English) "farmstead owner."

STEFAN: *see* Stephen.

STEIN: (German) "stone."

STEPHEN: (Greek) "crown; garland." Var. and dim., Stefan, Steffen, Steven; Steve, Stevie.

STERLING: (Teutonic) "good value; honest; genuine." Var., Stirling.

STERNE: (Middle English) "austere one."

STEVEN: *see* Stephen.

STEWART: (Anglo-Saxon) "keeper of the estate." Var. and dim., Stuart; Stew, Stu.

STILLMAN: (Anglo-Saxon) "quiet; gentle."

STINSON: (Old English) "son of stone."

STOCKLEY: (Old English) "from the stump meadow."

STOCKTON: (Old English) "from the stump town."

STOCKWELL: (Old English) "from the stump spring."

STODDARD: (Anglo-Saxon) "keeper of horses."

STOKE: (Middle English) "village."

STORM: (Old English) "tempest."

STORR: (Old Norse) "great one."

STOWE: (Old English) "from the place."

STRAHAN: (Irish Gaelic) "wise man."

STRATFORD: (Old English) "river ford on the street."

STRONG: (Old English) "powerful one."

STROUD: (Old English) "from the thicket."

STRUTHERS: (Irish Gaelic) "from the stream."

STUART: *see* Stewart.

STYLES: (Old English) "dweller by the stiles."

SUFFIELD: (Old English) "from the south field."

SULLIVAN: (Irish Gaelic) "black-eyed one."

SUMNER: (Latin) "one who summons and calls."

SUTCLIFF: (Old English) "from the south cliff."

SUTHERLAND: (Old Norse) "from the southern land."

SUTTON: (Anglo-Saxon) "from the south town" or "village."

SWAINE: (Teutonic) "boy." Var., Swain, Swane.

SWEENEY: (Irish Gaelic) "little hero."

SWINTON: (Old English) "dweller at the swine farm."

SYDNEY: *see* Sidney.

SYLVESTER: *see* Silas.

SYMINGTON: (Old English) "dweller at Simon's estate."

T

TAB: (Old German) "brilliant among the people."

TAD, THAD: *see* Theodore, Thaddeus.

TAFFY: (Old Welsh) "beloved one."

TAGGART: (Irish Gaelic) "son of the prelate."

TALBOTT: (Anglo-Saxon) "bloodhound." Var., Talbot, Tallboy.

TAM, TAMMANY, TOMAS: *see* Thomas.

TANNER: (Old English) "leather maker."

TANTON: (Old English) "from the quiet river town."

TARLETON: (Old English) "thunder ruler's estate."

TARRANT: (Old Welsh) "thunder."

TATE: (Teutonic) "cheerful." Var., Tait, Taite.

TAVIS: (Celtic) "son of David."

TAYLOR: (Latin) "the tailor."

TEAGUE: (Irish Gaelic) "post."

TEARLE: (Old English) "stern one."

TED, TEDDY: *see* Edward, Theodore, Theodoric.

TEDMOND: (Old English) "national protector."

TELFORD: (Old French) "iron-hewer."

TEMPLETON: (Old English) "temple town."

TENNYSON: (Middle English) "son of Dennis."

TERENCE: (Latin) "tender." Var. and dim., Terrence, Torrance; Torin, Terry.

TERRILL: (Teutonic) "belonging to Thor; martial."

TERRIS: (Old English) "son of Terrell or Terence."

TERRY: *see* Terence.

THADDEUS: (Hebrew) "praise to God." Dim., Tad, Thad.

THANE: (Old English) "warrior attendant."

THATCHER: (Anglo-Saxon) "a mender of roofs." Var., Thacher, Thackeray, Thaxter.

THAW: (Old English) "ice thaw."

THAYER: (Teutonic) "of the nation's army."

THEOBALD: *see* Tybalt.

THEODORE: (Greek) "gift of God." Var. and dim., Feodor, Feodore, Tudor; Dore, Tad, Ted, Teddie, Teddy, Theo.

THEODORIC: (Teutonic) "the people's ruler." Var. and dim., Derek, Derrick, Tedric; Derk, Ted, Teddie, Teddy.

THEON: (Greek) "godly."

THERON: (Greek) "a hunter."

THOMAS: (Hebrew) "the twin." Var. and dim., Tammany, Tomas; Tam, Tammy, Thom, Tom, Tommy.

THOR: (Scandinavian) "the thunderous one."

THORALD: (Old Norse) "thunder ruler."

THORBERT: (Old Norse) "thunder glorious."

THORBURN: (Old Norse) "thunder bear."

THORLEY: (Old English) "Thor's meadow."

THORMOND: (Old English) "Thor's protection."

THORNDYKE: (Old English) "from the thorny dike."

THORNE: (Old English) "dweller by a thorn tree."

THORNLEY: (Old English) "from the thorny meadow."

THORNTON: (Anglo-Saxon) "from the thorny place."

THORPE: (Anglo-Saxon) "from the small village."

THURLOW: (Old English) "of Thor's mountain." Var., Thorlow.

THURMAN: (Scandinavian) "under Thor's protection." Var., Thorman.

THURSTON: (Scandinavian) "Thor's jewel" or "stone."

TIERNAN: (Irish Gaelic) "master."

TIERNEY: (Irish Gaelic) "lordly one."

TILDEN: (Anglo-Saxon) "from a fertile valley."

TILFORD: (Old English) "from the liberal one's ford."

TILTON: (Old English) "from the liberal one's estate."

TIMON: (Greek) "reward, value."

TIMOTHY: (Greek) "honoring God." Dim., Tim, Timmie.

TITUS: (Latin) "safe; saved."

TOBIAS: (Hebrew) "God's goodness." Var. and dim., Tobit; Tobe, Toby.

TODD: (Latin) "the fox."

TOFT: (Old English) "a small farm."

TOLAND: (Old English) "owner of taxed land."

TOM, TOMAS, TOMMY: *see* Thomas.

TOMKIN: (Old English) "little Tom."

TONY: *see* Anthony.

TORMEY: (Irish Gaelic) "thunder spirit."

TORR: (Old English) "from the tower."

TORRANCE, TORIN: *see* Terence.

TOWNLEY: (Old English) "from the town meadow."

TOWNSEND: (Anglo-Saxon) "from the end of town."

TRACEY: (Anglo-Saxon) "the brave defender." Var., Tracey.

TRAHERN: (Old Welsh) "super strength."

TRAVERS: (Latin) "from the crossroad." Var., Travis.

TREDWAY: (Old English) "mighty warrior."

TREMAYNE: (Old Cornish) "dweller in the house at the rock."

TRENT: (Latin) "swift."

TREVELYAN: (Old Cornish) "from Elian's homestead."

TREVOR: (Celtic) "careful traveler."

TRIGG: (Old Norse) "trusty one."

TRISTAN: (Latin) "sorrowful."

TRISTRAM: (Latin-Welsh) "sorrowful labor."

TROWBRIDGE: (Old English) "dweller by the tree bridge."

TROY: (Old French) "at the place of the curly-haired people."

TRUE: (Old English) "faithful, loyal one."

TRUESDALE: (Old English) "from the beloved one's farmstead."

TRUMAN: (Anglo-Saxon) "a faithful man."

TRUMBLE: (Old English) "bold one."

TUCKER: (Middle English) "a tucker of cloth."

TUDOR: (Old Welsh) Welsh variation of Theodore.

TULLY: (Irish Gaelic) "quiet, peaceful one."

TUPPER: (Old English) "ram raiser."

TURNER: (Latin) "worker with the lathe."

TURPIN: (Old Norse) "thunder-Finn."

TUXFORD: (Old Norse-English) "ford of the national spearman."

TWAIN: (Middle English) "cut in two."

TWITCHELL: (Old English) "dweller on a narrow passage."

TWYFORD: (Old English) "from the double river ford."

TY: a dim. for any name beginning with "Ty."

TYBALT: (Teutonic) "leader of the people." Var. and dim., Theobald, Thibaut, Tybald; Ty.

TYLER: (Anglo-Saxon) "maker of tiles" or "bricks." Dim., Ty.

TYNAN: (Irish Gaelic) "dark or gray."

TYRONE: (Celtic) of uncertain meaning. Dim., Ty.

TYSON: (Teutonic) "son of the German." Dim., Sonny, Ty.

U

UDELL: (Old English) "from the yew tree valley."

UDOLF: (Old English) "prosperous wolf."

ULFRED: (Old English) "wolf peace."

ULGER: (Old English) "wolf spear."

ULLOCK: (Old English) "wolf sport."

ULMER: (Old Norse) "wolf famous."

ULRIC, ULRICH: *see* Alaric.

ULYSSES: (Greek) "angry one; wrathful."

UNNI: (Hebrew) "modest."

UPTON: (Anglo-Saxon) "from the hill town."

UPWOOD: (Old English) "from the upper forest."

URBAN: (Latin) "from the city; urbane; sophisticated."

URIAH: (Hebrew) "the Lord is my light." Var., Urias, Uriel.

UZIEL: (Hebrew) "a mighty force." Var., Uzziel.

V

VACHEL: (French) "keeper of the cattle." Var., Vachil.

VAIL: (Anglo-Saxon) "from the valley." Var., Vale, Valle.

VAL: (Teutonic) "might; power." Also dim. of any name beginning with "Val."

VALDEMAR: (Old German) "famous ruler."

VALENTINE: (Latin) "healthy; strong; valorous." Var., Valente, Valiant.

VALERIAN: (Latin) "strong; belonging to Valentine."

VANCE: (Dutch) "the son of a famous family." Var., Van.

VARIAN: (Latin) "clever; capricious."

VAUGHAN: (Celtic) "the small." Var., Vaughn, Von, Vonn.

VERE: (Latin) "true; faithful."

VERGE: (Anglo-French) "owner of a quarter-acre."

VERNON: (Latin) "growing green; flourishing." Var., Vern, Verne.

VERRILL: (Old French) "true one."

VICTOR: (Latin) "the conqueror." Var. and dim., Victoir, Vittorio; Vic, Vick.

VIGOR: (Latin) "vigor."

VINCENT: (Latin) "the conqueror." Dim., Vin, Vince.

VINSON: (Anglo-Saxon) "son of Vinn"; thus, "the conqueror's son."

VIRGIL: (Latin) "strong; flourishing." Var. and dim., Vergil; Virg, Virgie, Virgy.

VITO: (Latin) "vital."

VIVIEN: (Latin) "lively."

VLADIMIR: (Slavonic) "the ruler of all." Var. and dim., Vladamir, Waldemar, Wladimir; Vlad.

VLADISLAV: (Old Slavic) "glorious ruler."

VOLNEY: (Teutonic) "most popular." Var., Volny.

W

WACE: (Old English) "feudal tenant."

WADE: (Anglo-Saxon) "mover; wanderer."

WADLEY: (Old English) "the advancer's meadow."

WADSWORTH: (Old English) "from Wade's castle."

WAGNER: (German) "wagon maker."

WAINWRIGHT: (Old English) "wagon maker."

WAITE: (Middle English) "guard."

WAKE: (Old English) "watchful one."

WAKEFIELD: (Old English) "dweller at the wet field."

WAKELEY: (Old English) "from the wet field."

WAKEMAN: (Old English) "watchman."

WALBY: (Old English) "from the walled dwellings."

WALCOTT: (Anglo-Saxon) "cottage dweller."

WALDEMAR: (Teutonic) "strong; famous." Var. and dim., Waldimar; Waldo.

WALDEN: (Old English) "from the forest valley."

WALDO: (Old German) "ruler." *See also* Waldemar.

WALDRON: (Old German) "ruling raven."

WALFORD: (Old English) "from the Welshman's ford."

WALFRED: (Old German) "peaceful ruler."

WALKER: (Anglo-Saxon) "forest walker."

WALLACE: (Teutonic) "a foreigner." Var. and dim., Wallis, Walsh; Wallie, Wally.

WALLER: (Old English) "mason."

WALMOND: (Old German) "ruling protector."

WALSH: *see* Wallace.

WALTER: (Teutonic) "powerful; mighty warrior." Var. and dim., Walters; Wallie, Wally, Walt.

WALTON: (Old English) "dweller at the town by a ruined Roman wall."

WALWORTH: (Old English) "from the Welshman's farm."

WALWYN: (Old English) "Welsh friend."

WARBURTON: (Old English) "from the enduring castle town."

WARD: (Anglo-Saxon) "watchman; guardian." Var., Word.

WARDELL: (Old English) "from the watch hill."

WARDLEY: (Old English) "from the guardian's meadow."

WARE: (Anglo-Saxon) "always careful."

WARFIELD: (Middle English) "dweller at the field of the small stream dam."

WARFORD: (Middle English) "from the ford of the small stream dam."

WARING: (Anglo-Saxon) "the cautious soul."

WARLEY: (Middle English) "from the meadow of the small stream dam."

WARNER: (Teutonic) "protecting warrior."

WARREN: (Teutonic) "game warden."

WARRICK: (Teutonic) "strong ruler." Var., Aurick, Vareck, Varick.

WASHBURN: (Old English) "dweller at the flooding brook."

WASHINGTON: (Old English) "from the estate of the keen one's family."

WATFORD: (Old English) "from the hurdle ford."

WATKINS: (Old English) "son of Walter."

WATSON: (Anglo-Saxon) "warrior's son."

WAVERLY: (Old English) "quaking aspen-tree meadow."

WAYLAND: (Teutonic) "from the land near the highway."

WAYNE: (Teutonic) "wagon maker." Var., Waine, Wain.

WEBSTER: (Anglo-Saxon) "weaver." Dim., Web, Webb.

WEDDELL: (Old English) "dweller at the advancer's hill."

WELBORNE: (Old English) "dweller at the spring brook."

WELBY: (Scandinavian) "from the farm by the spring."

WELDON: (Teutonic) "from a hill near the well."

WELFORD: (Old English) "from the spring ford."

WELLS: (Old English) "from the springs."

WELTON: (Old English) "dweller at the spring town."

WENCESLAUS: (Old Slavic) "wreath of glory."

WENDELL: (Teutonic) "wanderer." Var., Wendel.

WENTWORTH: (Old English) "white one's estate."

WERNER: (Old German) "defending army."

WESCOTT: (Teutonic) "dwells at west cottage." Dim., Wes.

WESLEY: (Anglo-Saxon) "from the west meadow." Var. and dim., Wellesley; Wes.

WEST: (Old English) "man from the west."

WESTBROOK: (Old English) "from the west brook."

WESTBY: (Old English) "from the west farmstead."

WESTON: (Old English) "from the west estate."

WETHERBY: (Old English) "dweller at the wether(sheep) farm."

WETHERELL: (Old English) "from the corner where white sheep grazed in green pastures." (*wether*:sheep)

WETHERLY: (Old English) "dweller at the wether(sheep) meadow."

WHARTON: (Old English) "estate at the embankment."

WHEATLEY: (Old English) "wheat field."

WHEATON: (Old English) "wheat town."

WHEELER: (Old English) "wheel maker."

WHISTLER: (Old English) "piper."

WHITBY: (Old English) "from the white farmstead."

WHITCOMB: (Old English) "from the white hollow."

WHITELAW: (Anglo-Saxon) "of the white hill."

WHITFIELD: (Old English) "from the white field."

WHITFORD: (Old English) "from the white ford."

WHITLOCK: (Old English) "man with a white lock of hair."

WHITMAN: (Old English) "white-haired man."

WHITMORE: (Old English) "from the white moor."

WHITNEY: (Anglo-Saxon) "from a white island."

WHITTAKER: (Old English) "dweller at the white field."

WICKHAM: (Old English) "from the village meadow."

WICKLEY: (Old English) "village meadow."

WILBERT, WILBUR: *see* Gilbert.

WILFRED: (Teutonic) "firm peacemaker." Var. and dim., Wilfrid; Fred, Freddie.

WILL, WILLY: *see* William.

WILLARD: (Old English) "resolute and brave."

WILLIAM: (Teutonic) "determined protector." Var. and dim., Wilhelm, Willet, Willis; Bill, Billie, Billy, Will, Willy.

WILLOUGHBY: (Old English) "from the willow farm."

WILMER: (Old German) "famous, resolute one."

WILMOT: (Old German) "resolute spirit."

WILSON: (Teutonic) "son of William." Dim., Wil.

WILTON: (Old English) "from the spring farm."

WINCHELL: (Old English) "from a bend in a piece of land."

WINDSOR: (Old English) "boundary bank."

WINFIELD: (Anglo-Saxon) "from the friendly field."

WINGATE: (Old English) "divine protection."

WINIFRED: (Teutonic) "friend of peace." Var. and dim., Winfred, Winfrid; Fred, Win.

WINSLOW: (Teutonic) "from the friendly hill." Dim., Win.

WINSTON: (Anglo-Saxon) "from the friendly town." Var. and dim., Winton; Win.

WINTER: (Old English) "born in winter."

WINTHROP: (Teutonic) "from the friendly village."

WINTON: (Old English) "from the friend's estate."

WINWARD: (Old English) "friend's forest."

WIRT: (German) "master."

WITT: (Old English) "wise man."

WITTER: (Old English) "wise warrior."

WITTON: (Old English) "from the wise man's estate."

WOLCOTT: (Old English) "from wolf's cottage."

WOLFE: (Teutonic) "a wolf."

WOLFGANG: (Old German) "advancing wolf."

WOLFRAM: (Teutonic) "respected; feared."

WLADIMIR: *see* Vladimir.

WOODLEY: (Anglo-Saxon) "from the wooded meadow."

WOODROW: (Anglo-Saxon) "from the hedgerow in the wood." Dim., Woodie.

WOODRUFF: (Old English) "forest warden."

WOODWARD: (Old English) "forester."

WORCESTER: (Old English) "alder forest army camp."

WORD: *see* Ward.

WORDSWORTH: (Old English) "wolf guardian's farm."

WORTH: (Old English) "farmstead."

WORTON: (Old English) "dweller at the vegetable enclosure."

WRAY: (Old Norse) "from the corner property."

WREN: (Old Welsh) "chief."

WRIGHT: (Anglo-Saxon) "craftsman; worker."

WYATT: (French) "a guide." *See also* Guy.

WYBORN: (Old Norse) "war bear."

WYCLIFF: (Old English) "from the white cliff."

WYLIE: (Anglo-Saxon) "beguiling; charming."

WYMAN: (Old English) "warrior."

WYMER: (Old English) "famous in battle."

WYNDHAM: (Old English) "from the enclosure with the winding path."
WYNN: (Old Welsh) "white one." *See also* Elwin.
WYTHE: (Middle English) "dweller at the willow tree."

XAVIER: (Arabic) "bright." Var., Javier.
XENOS: (Greek) "stronger."
XERXES: (Persian) "king."
XYLON: (Greek) "from the forest."

YALE: (Teutonic) "payer; yielder."
YANCY: (French) "Englishman." Var., Yancey.
YATES: (Anglo-Saxon) "the gate dweller" or "protector."
YEHUDI: (Hebrew) "the praise of the Lord."
YEOMAN: (Middle English) "retainer."
YORK: (Latin) "sacred tree." Var., Yorick, Yorke.
YULE: (Old English) "born at Christmas."
YVES: (Scandinavian) "an archer." Var., Ives, Yvon.

Z

ZACHARIAH: (Hebrew) "the Lord's remembrance." Var. and dim., Zacharias, Zachary; Zach, Zack.

ZACHARY: *see* Zachariah.

ZADOK: (Hebrew) "righteous one."

ZANE: *see* John.

ZARED: (Hebrew) "ambush."

ZEBADIAH: (Hebrew) "the Lord's gift." Var. and dim., Zebedee; Zebe, Zeb.

ZEBULON: (Hebrew) "dwelling place." Dim., Lonny, Zeb.

ZEDEKIAH: (Hebrew) "justice of the Lord."

ZEEMAN: (Dutch) "seaman."

ZEKE: *see* Ezekiel.

ZELIG: (Teutonic) "blessed." Var., Selig.

ZELOTES: (Greek) "zealous one."

ZENAS: (Greek) "Jupiter's gift."

ZEPHANIAH: (Hebrew) "hidden by the Lord." Dim., Zeph.

ZEUS: (Greek) "living one."

ZIV: (Old Slavic) "living one."

ZURIEL: (Hebrew) "God; my rock."

YOUR BABY'S

HOROSCOPE

A guide to his or her personality traits; traditional birthstones; traditional flowers; traditional colors.

SIGNS OF THE ZODIAC

CAPRICORN	Dec. 22-Jan. 20
AQUARIUS	Jan. 21-Feb 19
PISCES	Feb. 20-Mar. 20
ARIES	Mar. 21-Apr. 20
TAURUS	Apr. 21-May 21
GEMINI	May 22-June. 21
CANCER	Jun. 22-Jul. 23
LEO	Jul. 24-Aug. 23
VIRGO	Aug. 24-Sept. 23
LIBRA	Sept. 24-Oct.23
SCORPIO	Oct. 24-Nov. 22
SAGITTARIUS	Nov. 23-Dec. 21

BABIES BORN UNDER THE SIGN OF

Capricorn

(DECEMBER 22–JANUARY 20)

The Most Conscientious Children of the Zodiac

Perhaps you will be annoyed when these children are not willing to make friends with children of their own age. Probably you won't understand why they prefer to pick their few friends among older boys and girls. Perhaps you will try to argue with them about it, with the result that they "withdraw in their shell" and become even more self-conscious and solitary. Don't scold them for being shy or sullen, as it may seem to you. They are never "good mixers." They have mental resources within themselves and often prefer their own company to that of other children, especially those who seem "babyish" to the more mature-minded Capricorn children. Why not guide this intelligence constructively by giving them some tasks at which they may be of service to you? They can be depended upon to discharge any task given them with more thoroughness and patience than most children. They are not the ones to quit in the middle of a task; they finish whatever they begin.

You need not worry about how they will get along in their schoolwork either, for they are inclined to study hard and put into practical use the knowledge that they gain. Not infrequently, you will find them interested in some line of study leading to a trade or a profession. They will be ambitious to get to the top of the field and have the patience to build their success on a firm foundation of lessons well learned. Don't, however, expect them to be hail-fellows-well-met. Never will they aspire to be cheerleaders of the football team. If they have anything to do with the team, it will probably be as business managers, not star players.

Saturn's influence as ruler of Capricorn bestows the valuable qualities of efficiency, levelheadedness, and conscientiousness to these children; but it also fosters a tendency toward pessimism unless direct effort is made to prevent such development. You can be very helpful in teaching them to find the brighter side of life rather than to dwell on the darker side. Diligence, stability, and practicality are key words assigned to the children born under Capricorn. This does not indicate, however, that they crave only responsibilities and duties in their lives. There is the natural enjoyment of fun in their makeup which needs to be brought out for an airing every so often. See that there is time set aside regularly for recreational indulgences in order that they may develop a well-rounded personality.

Capricorn—with its ruler, Saturn—has dominion over the bones, outer layer of the skin, joints, and the hardening processes of the body. These children must guard against disorders which can result from their tendency to become despondent. You must teach them to transcend this untoward potential by seeing to it that they have a warm, comfortable, and congenial home; nourishing food; and sufficient physical exercise to keep their minds in healthy functioning condition at all times.

BABIES BORN UNDER THE SIGN OF

Aquarius

(JANUARY 21—FEBRUARY 19)

The Most Loyal Children of the Zodiac

These children do not enjoy solitude. Companionships are important to them, however young or old they may be. As their parent, you will be wise to make chums or companions of them rather than assume the role of stern master, for these children, on the whole, do not need strict discipline and are more obedient to your wishes than children of most of the other signs. You may be sure that they will ask more than the usual number of questions, for they will want to know the reason that they should not play with matches or put a negative and positive electric wire together, but once you have explained to them that matches can cause fires or phosphorus poisoning and that positive and negative currents blow out fuses when they meet, you will find them willing to forego the experiments they would otherwise make.

In their search for companionship, they will prefer to be with those who are older than they are. Their intelligence will be above the average child of their age, and since they are agreeable companions, the chief danger is that they will be spoiled with too much attention and allowed too many privileges for their years.

One of the best means of development for these children is through caring for pets. You can give them great happiness by bringing home a stray kitten or a puppy. Pets which require outdoor care or exercise will also serve to take these children out of doors more than they would be otherwise, for their natural tendency is to prefer indoor activities or reading. They are naturally ambitious to learn and to open to themselves the avenues of culture and recognition to which education is the gate. Their ambition is more to "be someone" than to accumulate material possessions, and education is, to them, a means to this end.

Since Aquarius is the sign which rules the blood stream, infections caused by diseased tonsils or bad teeth are not infrequently the cause of illness in children of this sign. Aquarius also rules the ankles; sprained ankles are a frequent accident. But you won't have to bandage many broken knuckles or doctor many black eyes, for they aren't the ones to look for fights or participate in them if they can avoid it. Their nature is, on the whole, inclined toward shyness, and they are more disposed to yield to the opinion of others if doing so secures harmony. Their friendships, when formed, are likely to be lasting, since they will never be the first to break up an existing condition. This fixed and constant nature also results in a certain amount of stubbornness, and you will find them easier to control by affection than by force. In planning their education, philosophy, science, and literature are lines in which they will take the greatest interest. There is frequently inventive ability along scientific lines, and they will also find great interest in humanitarian work. These children rarely lead what would be called a dull life, and this is shared naturally by family and friends.

BABIES BORN UNDER THE SIGN OF

Pisces

(FEBRUARY 20–MARCH 20)

The Most Imaginative Children of the Zodiac

If you are given to mottos, the best one you can tack up for the Pisces children is that about bad companions corrupting good morals, for they are more susceptible to the influence of their playmates, for good or evil. The reason for this is that Pisces is a negative sign, extremely sensitive to any influence around it and with less than the usual power to resist these influences. It is, therefore, up to you to see that they do not come under unfavorable influences until they are old enough to be able to know right from wrong.

Their easygoing, self-indulgent nature makes them exceedingly fond of rich foods—and with a strong tendency to drink. These disastrous tendencies have more chance to be indulged because these children are agreeable, sympathetic, kind, and friendly, and, therefore, much sought after as companions. Unless they are taught self-control along these lines, they may not only ruin their lives but ruin their health as well.

If a restraining and constructive influence is brought to

151

bear upon them, however, you will find them developing into idealistic, amiable, imaginative, and orderly young persons. They are capable of acquiring a good education; and because of their agreeable disposition, they will cause little trouble to their teachers. They are not ones to seek fights—in fact, they are so inclined to peaceful measures that they will often allow others to impose upon them rather than start fights.

You may trust them to keep secrets, for in spite of their talkativeness, they are dependable and honest and seldom betray any trusts reposed in them. Their lack of physical energy, however, will make them averse to hard work, and they may shrink from household chores assigned to them, but if you insist upon this work, you will find that they do it in an effortless and methodical way—probably in order to make it as easy for themselves as possible. Training in distasteful tasks during the early years will be excellent discipline for them. Don't think it unusual if they spend hours in daydreaming; Neptune, their ruling planet, is irresponsible, mystic, and romantic, and his children show all of these qualities. Because of their sensitive nature, they will be confused and hurt by a reprimand rather than resentful, and they may feel very sorry for themselves when you punish them. The things they fail to do rather than those they do will be your chief cause for complaint against them. You will find them forgetful, careless about picking up after themselves, neglectful of their possessions, and not very attentive to your instructions—usually because they are daydreaming of something a thousand miles away. Don't be lacking in understanding and sympathy for them; on the other hand, don't coddle them or fight their battles for them—their greatest need is to develop will power and self-confidence in order to be prepared to face life and its problems. They need a sturdy anchor early in life lest they become mental wanderers.

BABIES BORN UNDER THE SIGN OF

Aries

(MARCH 21–APRIL 20)

The Most Brilliant Children of the Zodiac

As parents of an Aries child, you may become prematurely gray worrying about what hair-raising stunt they will try next, whether their last bump will subside before they raise another and whether any head can be injured as many times as theirs and still function properly. In Aries children, you will have a bundle of Mars (their ruler) energy, enthusiasm, and dynamic power ready to explode at any—or without any—provocation. Their vitality is so abundant that they just must be doing something all the time, and usually it is something which requires physical expression.

They are born leaders—and born fighters, and if they do not play at fighting, they fight at playing! They are venturesome to the extent of foolhardiness, and when an idea occurs to them—as it does with more than the usual frequency of childish ideas—they never stop to figure out the consequences of their action.

Aside from the physical restraint which they need, they must be taught moderation in personal conduct, in speech, and in their personal outlook upon life. They are never "shrinking violets" and self-assertion, rather than self-consciousness, is their chief characteristic.

The energy and enthusiasm of Aries children may make them hard workers and able to earn money, but they will be very poor savers. They are not very good at sticking to a task once their enthusiasm has worn off. The qualities of leadership are manifested in their relations with their playmates, for Aries children can get more work out of them than they would ever do of their own accord. This very power of leadership makes Aries children a great force for either good or evil, and if their energy is misdirected, they can become gang leaders instead of leaders for the cause of justice and order. It is essential that this powerful nature be directed from childhood into the right paths.

The emotional nature of Aries children is ardent, demonstrative, and frequently idealistic. They are happy to feel themselves the champions of the weaker and less fortunate. Cultivate in them this sense of responsibility for others, and, above everything else, try to teach them to stick to one job until they have finished it, and not to scatter their enthusiasm over a multitude of projects.

The nature of Mars and the mental qualities of Aries are manifested in these children's hasty speech, quick temper, enthusiasm, quick wit, and love of freedom. They are the pioneers in the new undertakings, and they will find their greatest success in executive positions where their aggressiveness and superabundant energy will have the fullest scope possible.

In matters of health, aside from accidents caused by the recklessness and daring which are so typical, there is danger of fevers, headaches, and kidney ailments. For these children, adequate rest and relaxation are requisites for maintenance of health, for they are inclined to use up vitality faster than they can generate it.

BABIES BORN UNDER THE SIGN OF

Taurus

(APRIL 21–MAY 21)

The Most Popular Children of the Zodiac

You will find that Taurus children are never carried away by wild enthusiasms, nor will they dash away to follow any leader who would be accepted by less stable and strong-willed children. They resemble the patient bull, who must be annoyed and tormented before aroused to anger. But, as you may know, once a bull decides to fight, he makes a thorough and complete job of it. Taurus children do the same.

Unless Taurus children are actually tormented until their patient nature can endure no more, however, they will be reluctant to fight—partly because they are naturally slow to act and partly because they abhor pain—and fights usually result in a missing tooth or two. Their nature is fundamentally gentle, and you may, with proper handling, manage them for years without seeing any evidence of anger or temper. You will never forget it, though, if their temper is aroused, for under these conditions, they are not only furious and headstrong, but stubborn in yielding to the opinion or authority of others. But on the whole, they will give you far less to worry about than most other children.

Their natural secretiveness adds to their reserved nature, but their practical and constructive qualities offset the less friendly characteristics. Music, art, literature, and all the beauty of nature will appeal to them. In speech or writing, however, they may be somewhat inarticulate. They feel strongly, but express themselves with difficulty. The practical and conservative side of their nature will show itself in their love of home and birthplace. In their friendships, they are both faithful and warm-hearted. They are, however, much more easily hurt than one would believe from their self-sufficient and somewhat too confident manner. Unless they are praised, loved, and encouraged, they tend to become indifferent and will underrate their own abilities. Praise them, but don't indulge them. Don't let them take life too easy, for this indifference could develop into actual laziness. Keep a keen eye on their natural inclination to overeat, especially since this fondness for good things tends to lead in later life to congestion of the kidneys, enlargement of the liver, heart disease, and rheumatism—all results of overindulgence of the appetite. Conditions affecting the throat are specially marked in those born under Taurus.

Their mind is steady, unimaginative, slow in action but extremely fixed when that action has finally developed. In brief, they are the perfect example of the conservative virtues—"slow but sure" and "haste makes waste." Their appreciation of the material blessings of this world will tend to make them strive to accumulate the means to purchase comfort and pleasure—two things which they consider most important in their scheme of life. Sometimes they secure these comforts and pleasures as rewards of their own thrift, sometimes as a legacy; in any case, their material lot in life is more fortunate than average.

BABIES BORN UNDER THE SIGN OF

Gemini

(MAY 22–JUNE 21)

The Most Alert Children of the Zodiac

Only the parents of twins can appreciate the problem that falls to the parents of Gemini children. For Gemini is the sign of the twins, and Gemini children will frequently represent such a "split personality" that they do not understand even their own nature or know what they actually want from life. One of the best things you can do for them is to teach them, when young, to stick to one line, instead of trying to carry on two or more interests.

These children are inclined to lack concentration and to "talk your ear off." They are the ones who are told that "children should be seen and not heard"—probably because they make themselves heard more than any other member of the family. But you should realize that they possess a high-strung, highly organized nervous system. Unnecessary talk, in either children or adults, is a sign of overtaxed nerves, as well as strain on the nerves of those who must listen.

Part of the constant questioning of these children is due to

157

an actual desire for information, for they are always quick-witted and bright, but their curiosity is rather superficial. They want to know something about everything that happens to cross their path, but they will not persist in one line of thought long enough to learn much on any subject or stick to one task or one line of work long enough to make an outstanding success of it. They have a quick, active, and curious mind, and they will constantly look for change. Because they are adaptable, they do not hesitate to try new roads. Your problem will be to keep them on the old road long enough to "get somewhere."

Another point to keep in mind in understanding these children is that their bodies need stimulation much more than their minds do. Let them do the active physical things which will give an outlet for their nervous energy, but keep them mentally calm. Do not, unless you want children with "nerves" that will prove a real detriment in later years, tell them bedtime stories of Bluebeard or Jack the Giant Killer, for their overwrought imagination will work even in sleep, and you will be awakened by their terrified "nightmares," in which the giant is pursuing them. Put them to bed early, for they need sleep, and let nothing in their minds disturb their rest, for they need all they can get. Even afternoon naps are excellent to quiet their nerves—and probably yours, too!

In spite of their highly organized nervous system, and general lack of robustness, they will seldom suffer from serious illness with the exception of lung trouble, a disease to which they are especially subject, since Gemini rules the lungs. In accidents, the hands, arms, and shoulders, all under Gemini, are most apt to be the points of injury, with the intestines, feet, and thighs the other points through which sickness may work out. On the whole, however, their nerves and yours will give you most of your problems!

BABIES BORN UNDER THE SIGN OF

Cancer

(JUNE 22-JULY 23)

The Most Sensitive Children of the Zodiac

These children, during early years, are inclined to be somewhat weak physically. Along with their lack of robust health, they show an extremely sensitive emotional nature. They are easily hurt by an unkind word, and so responsive to the conditions around them that they can actually become ill by association with unhealthy or weak nurses or governesses. Because of their affectionate nature, they crave praise and love, but they are slow to show this because of a natural modesty and reticence. There is also a tendency to brood over fancied slights or injuries, more so than will be found in other children. They are, however, extremely unselfish and so lacking in aggressiveness that other children frequently impose upon them. While they are not inclined to fight for their rights and actually feel and fear pain more than those with less sensitive natures, they have one valuable characteristic which serves well when they are forced to defend themselves—the crab's tenacity and determination to hang on to the bitter end when they have been aroused to defend their rights.

Children born under this sign have a true spirit of patriotism and pride in their country and their home. You will hear them telling their playmates that their family is the best and their father is the most important man in town, for that's the way they feel about those who are dear to them. They will appreciate their home and stay in it more than most other children.

Do not make many sacrifices to send these children through college unless they show some unusual ability, for their best school is Experience, and they learn more from people, travel, and experience than from any academic education. They will have a natural inclination to travel. And the ups and downs of life which come to most of these children are all lessons that no school could teach. In matters of health, watch their stomachs. Cancer is the sign ruling this part of the body, and unless they rule their stomachs and control their craving for the wrong kind of food, their stomachs will rule—or ruin—them. Don't let them be "fussy" about their meals, but see that they eat plain and nourishing foods and not too much of any kind, for the digestion is inclined to be delicate. Don't expose them to contagious diseases, for they are as receptive to germs as is butter to fish odors when the two are neighbors in the refrigerator. And don't try Spartan methods of discipline, for Cancer children are better ruled by love and encouragement, and will never do their best in an atmosphere of disapproval.

These children are usually mild-mannered and somewhat kind in their reaction to persons other than those with whom they are closely associated. Assurance of acceptance and a feeling of security are very necessary to their well-being. They have a strong attachment to the mother and home, which usually continues throughout life. World activities make an unusually profound impression on these children, who generally are very much in tune with what is taking place on this earthly sphere.

BABIES BORN UNDER THE SIGN OF

Leo

(JULY 24-AUGUST 23)

The Happiest Children of the Zodiac

These children want to be the center of attention—favorable attention, of course. They thrive on adulation; they demand praise for all that they do, and they will do a surprising amount under the stimulus of "That's fine. You are wonderful." They are more responsive to love and tenderness than to punishment. If you find fault with them, they will become irritable and indifferent. As they grow up, that motto of kings, *"noblesse oblige"* (nobility imposes obligation), will bring out the finest qualities in them—nobility, generosity, self-reliance, leadership, pride, and magnanimity.

In talking to them, remember to be exact in your statements and to mean what you say as well as say what you mean, for they not only understand more than many children their age, but they remember your promises. They will tend to imitate the morals and manners of older persons with whom they associate, so pick their companions with care, and see that the books they read are those which preserve the naturally high Leo ideals. They love adventure and their naturally idealistic mind will delight in stories of noble deeds.

They are natural organizers, delighting in positions of responsibility, and their good nature and ability to mix will fit them for many lines of work in which they contact the public. They are not natural students or very much inclined toward hard manual work, but the artistic and musical qualities natural to Leo will sometimes produce very successful artists in various lines.

These children will not stoop to low or mean action, even at great profit to themselves. No sacrifice is too great for them to make for anyone they love. They act from motives of the heart, not the brain, and are quickly moved by an emotional appeal. They are better leaders than followers; and in children's games, you may have to watch them to see that they do not insist upon leading the game all the time, to their ultimate unpopularity with the gang. Also, do not believe all that they tell you. Their tales have the basis of truth, and they do not lie deliberately, but this inclination will add four more inches on the distance they can jump or a grand aspect to anything they have done.

While these children are quick-tempered, they are equally quick to forgive and their magnanimous nature makes them willing to apologize readily and forgive and forget. They have no bitter enemies, for their hearts seldom find room for hate.

Do not expect them to save their pennies, for theirs is not a saving nature, and their natural tendency to be overoptimistic leads them to think that more pennies will be forthcoming, so they share what they have with the less fortunate with a lordly indifference to the future.

They have unusual vitality; under ordinary conditions, they are seldom sick. There is some tendency to heart trouble, since Leo rules the heart, and to disorders of the blood and some conditions affecting the spine, but on the whole their health is robust and their disposition delightful.

BABIES BORN UNDER THE SIGN OF

Virgo

(AUGUST 24-SEPTEMBER 23)

The Most Ambitious Children of the Zodiac

Virgo children, above all others, should be given every opportunity for a thorough and complete education. Otherwise, when they grow up, they will be very unhappy to find themselves less equipped mentally than those with whom they associate. They have a natural thirst for knowledge and put great stress upon little things—upon saying the right things and doing the right things—right, for them, meaning correct rather than ethical.

These children have an interest in any subject which they take up and study for the sheer pleasure of acquiring knowledge. They make high grades in school, give the teachers little or no trouble, but may be unknown to most of their schoolmates because of their indifferences to companions and their lack of inclination to "mix" with their fellow students. They are not inclined to seek leadership in games or to push themselves forward for class offices; and while almost always good students, they will tend to remain in the background socially because of lack of interest in making friends.

Order and routine are natural and pleasing to them, and you will never need to complain that they don't pick up their clothes or put away their books or keep their rooms in order. On the other hand, they will probably make everyone who associates with them miserable by insisting that they keep things in the same neat fashion that is second nature to them.

The tendency to be critical of those who are less perfect in behavior than themselves, and to find fault with all the smaller sins and shortcomings of humanity, is one of the worst characteristics to be found in Virgo children. Their motto, whether they are old enough to express it or not, is "Trifles make perfection, but perfection is no trifle," but in their effort to attain it they are inclined "to strain out gnats and swallow camels," as the saying goes. They put so much stress upon small matters that they are unprepared to meet the larger issues, and small disappointments loom so huge in their mind that they are hardly prepared to meet the real tragedies that come into every life at some time. Try, if possible, to develop their sense of proportion in life, and to overcome their natural tendency to be fussy and fretful about trifles.

These children will appreciate a good environment. They are inclined to want to better themselves both socially and financially, and will work hard if they see that their efforts will be rewarded. Diet, hygiene, and science are subjects that interest them.

While they are somewhat quick-tempered and "fussy," they are not inclined to fight, and they seldom act upon anything without deliberation and forethought. They are, therefore, less likely to get into difficulties than the more impulsive and aggressive children.

As far as illness goes, intestinal complaints are the chief causes of poor health, but never let them get into the habit of thinking themselves invalids, for they can "enjoy poor health" to a remarkable degree, and actually intensify their condition by worrying about it.

BABIES BORN UNDER THE SIGN OF

Libra

(SEPTEMBER 24-OCTOBER 23)

The Most Intuitive Children of the Zodiac

These children, more than any others, show artistic tendencies at an early age. They are graceful and attractive when children of other signs are awkward and self-conscious. They are the ones who are called upon by a fond teacher to sing solos on the last day of school or draw the cover of the school magazine, and their popularity is such that less attractive and fortunate children "turn green with envy." There is a reason for this popularity beyond their ability to "show off" to advantage in any artistic field. They are extremely easy to get along with; and in association with children of stronger will, they can be counted on to give in and let the others have things their way—which, of course, makes for popularity. It is, however, an undesirable quality for future development, for above everything else, they need to develop will power—the will to stick to whatever they start until they have made a success of it. Therefore, begin early in life to impress them with the fact that success in any field, artistic or otherwise, is one-third talent and two-thirds the will power to stick to whatever they start until they get to the top. In other words, don't let them be dilettantes who fritter away talents and accomplishments that might be a source of livelihood in life.

They have a natural apathy which is not far from being actual indolence, unless it is overcome in early life. They like to slide through life as easily as possible; and when work interferes with pleasure they are more than willing to sidetrack the work.

In spite of the fact that Venus, planet of the emotions, is the ruler of Libra, these children are not especially responsive to affection and are apt to appear cold and indifferent to the attention of admirers. They are lovable, have a pleasing way about them, but they lack the fighting qualities which they need to make a place for themselves in the world.

If you should find that Libra children want to become dancers when you want them to become schoolteachers or bookkeepers, you will be wise to give up the idea of fitting "square pegs into round holes" and instead give them every encouragement to become a success in the career of their choice. Just see to it that they stick to the career for which they are best suited. The enthusiasm with which they start out is not always a guarantee that the asborbing interest will continue, for they are ardent in anything they do—until something else attracts them, and they switch their energy into a new field.

This changing enthusiasm is no less a characteristic of Libra children than the tendency to swing from the heights of optimism to the depths of melancholy without any adequate reason. While Libra is represented by the balance, or scales, the tendency is to swing to extremes in seeking that balance, and Libra is perhaps more marked in these changing moods than any other sign.

They are quick-tempered, but not inclined to hold spite. The danger is that they will become too pliant. Will power and stick-to-itiveness are the qualities they will need most of all.

BABIES BORN UNDER THE SIGN OF

Scorpio

(OCTOBER 24-NOVEMBER 22)

The Most Thorough Children of the Zodiac

Children born under this sign of the Zodiac will put the worried parent in the same spot as the driver of a dynamite truck. If you get it where it is going, it may be usefully employed blasting out rocks and destroying outmoded structures, to make way for other finer new developments. If you don't and another truck crashes into it and explodes it prematurely, the resulting damage is terrible to contemplate. "Dynamic"—akin to dynamite in its explosive power—is the word often associated with Scorpio personalities. These children must have, somewhere or somehow, constructive outlets for the energy they possess, or they will, at the most inopportune moment, explode with destructive force which, as often as not, takes shape in physical violence.

Moderation is a word that is practically unknown to these children; and half measures, to them, are worse than none. They are either all for something or someone, or so bitterly against it that no force or argument can sway them. They are natural fighters, always ready to take up an argument either on their own behalf or for some less aggressive comrade to whom they have given their loyalty. Their motto is never "Peace at any price"—rather it is "War on any provocation." If they are not in physical conflict for material gain, they are in verbal conflict for a cause which they believe to be right.

They can be sarcastic in speech and display a quick-flashing temper, so it is essential in early life to take them in hand and teach them self-control. This will not be an easy task, for they have an unusual amount of determination and do not obey without knowing the reason for doing so. Reason with them and treat them as companions, not as inferiors, and you will find them responsive and loyal. The more straightforward and frank you are in your relations with them, the better you will be able to handle them and the more they will respect you.

Selfishness and self-preservation are dominant Scorpio characteristics, so you need not worry that these children will not be able to look out for themselves and get their share of the world's goods—and a part of the other fellow's share, usually. A shrewd and penetrating mentality makes them quick and intelligent students, especially skilled in mechanical matters.

An unusual amount of physical energy, great recuperative power, and a robust constitution make these children recover quickly from feverish illnesses. Care should be taken in teaching them sex hygiene, as the sun in Scorpio stimulates the generative and eliminative functions and necessitates unusual moral and physical cleanliness. Sex is very frequently a problem with them, and it is the wise parent who approaches the matter honestly, intelligently, and early. These children lost their illusions about the stork almost as soon as they learn that there is no Santa Claus, so you might as well face the fact and provide an intelligent explanation for them.

BABIES BORN UNDER THE SIGN OF

Sagittarius

(NOVEMBER 23-DECEMBER 21)

The Most Independent Children of the Zodiac

These children are not only hopeful and trusting, but gay and light of heart. High-mindedness, truthfulness, and a natural lack of selfishness are some of the finer qualities which may be expected of them. They are not, however, natural students or much inclined to sit quietly indoors and read. They would rather be outdoors—riding, skating, sledding, or engaged in some active sport. Try to see to it that they are never without pets of some kind, for living "playthings" are much more to their liking than inanimate toys.

Don't blanket their natural enthusiasm, for it is a quality worthy of cultivation; but direct it, if you wish, along constructive and useful channels. You might be wise to teach them, before they learn from painful experience, that they are not to believe all that they hear, as their own truthful nature makes them believe that everyone with whom they deal will be just as honest. They are slow to understand that others are less honest and aboveboard than they would be in like circumstances. They judge others by their own high standards, and they lack suspiciousness because they have none of the qualities which arouse it in themselves. In your own relations with them, show appreciation of their trustworthiness by giving them all possible freedom. Make chums or companions of them instead of giving them military orders, for they are hard to drive but easy to guide. In the matter of education, let them follow their own inclinations, for their ambitions may range from the ministry through law, or into work that brings them in contact with horses, dogs, and various types of sports.

They will have more than the usual amount of childish curiosity, also, and they will not only ask many questions but may be very analytical and critical of the shortcomings of their family group. Needless to say, such outspoken opinions could be very upsetting, so don't try to stand too much on your dignity with these children. They will obey readily enough if they feel that your request is fair and your explanation to them is truthful. Their tendency to tease, however, is a habit that should be curbed early in life, as it becomes increasingly annoying as they grow older. Another bad habit is that of making promises in an effort to please and then failing to keep them. Patience is a virtue which they will need to cultivate, since they seldom have it, but on the whole, their faults are minor ones.

Derangement of the nervous system which results from the habit of living too actively is one of the illnesses from which they may suffer, and accidents to the hips (governed by Sagittarius), hands, and joints are not unusual. Their unusual amount of reserve force, however, gives better than average health. One of the best ways to keep them well is to allow them to indulge their natural enthusiasms, for suppression and restriction are both mentally and physically harmful to them.

TRADITIONAL
BIRTHSTONES
of
THE ZODIAC

Capricorn	Ruby, Chalcedony
Aquarius	Garnet, Amethyst
Pisces	Amethyst
Aries	Bloodstone, Crystal
Taurus	Sapphire, Ruby, Diamond
Gemini	Agate, Sapphire, Quartz
Cancer	Emerald, Cat's-eye, Moonstone
Leo	Onyx, Amber, Topaz, Tourmaline
Virgo	Carnelian, Jade, Magnetic Stones
Libra	Peridot, Aquamarine, Garnet
Scorpio	Topaz
Sagittarius	Emerald, Topaz

TRADITIONAL FLOWERS *of* **THE ZODIAC**

Capricorn	Flaxweed, Moss, Rush, Ivy, Amaranth
Aquarius	Daffodil, Pansy
Pisces	Tuberose, Water Lily, Lotus
Aries	Buttercup, Daisy, Starthistle
Taurus	Cowslip, Daisy, Goldenrod, Violet
Gemini	Marigold, Fern, Lily-of-the-Valley
Cancer	Iris, Lily, White Poppy, White Rose
Leo	Poppy, Peony, Sunflower, Red Rose
Virgo	Fern, Lavender, Azalea, Morning Glory
Libra	Goldenrod, Violet, Cowslip, Nasturtium
Scorpio	Thistle, Hawthorn, Honeysuckle, Anemone
Sagittarius	Holly, Jessamine, Carnation, Chrysanthemum

TRADITIONAL COLORS *of* THE ZODIAC

Capricorn . . . . Dark Browns, Green, Black
Aquarius . . . . Mingled Shades, Stripes, Plaids
Pisces . . . . . Green-Blue, Shades of Lavender, Amethyst
Aries . . . . Brilliant Red
Taurus . . . . Red-Orange, Yellow, Cream
Gemini . . . . Mixed and Spotted, Silvery Gray, Blue
Cancer . . . . Delicate Greens, Pearl, Opalescent Shades
Leo . . . . Amber, Deep Orange, Golden Yellow
Virgo . . . . Yellow, Grayish Blue
Libra . . . Pale Blue to Deep Blue, Pale Yellow, Pastels
Scorpio . . . . Deep Red
Sagittarius . . . . Rich Deep Violet-Blue